THE PHILOSOPHY OF RELIGION

Swami Krishnananda

Published By

THE DIVINE LIFE SOCIETY

P.O. SHIVANANDANAGAR—249 192

Distt. Tehri-Garhwal, U.P., Himalayas, India

Price]   1997   [Rs. 50/-

First Edition : 1985
Second Edition : 1997
(3,000 Copies)

©The Divine Life Trust Society

ISBN 81-7052-132-7

Published by Swami Krishnananda for The Divine Life Society,
Shivanandanagar, and printed by him at the Yoga-Vedanta
Forest Academy Press, P.O. Shivanandanagar,
Distt. Tehri-Garhwal, U.P., Himalayas, India

PREFACE

The present publication consists of another series of lectures addressed by the author to the students of the Academy at the Headquarters of The Divine Life Society. Though the book is indeed going to be a useful and interesting reading, it may not equally be an easy reading. As the themes advance through the chapters, there is a tendency in the presentation to become a little more difficult gradually, mainly on account of the nature of the subjects treated in the later sections. This is especially so with the second half of the book, which enters into a discussion of varied topics, theoretical as well as practical. The last chapter may require a specially concentrated attention of the student, in the light of the novelty of the approach to the subject.

This valued contribution may with advantage be studied as a fitting sequel to the author's earlier "An Introduction to the Philosophy of Yoga" and "Yoga as a Universal Science". The three texts read in a sequence would form almost a complete exposition of the vast range of the foundations as well as the practical methodology of the human quest for eternal values.

Shivanandanagar,   THE DIVINE LIFE SOCIETY
1st March, 1997

CONTENTS

CHAPTER VIII

CHAPTER IX

CHAPTER X

CHAPTER XI

CHAPTER XII

THE PHILOSOPHY
OF
RELIGION

Chapter I

INTRODUCTION

The Seed of Philosophy

When anyone decides to make a trip to a holy place or visit a saint, he must be having a feeling within him of some sort of an inadequacy about the place where he is living and the circumstances under which he is working. This perception, which makes one take this decision, may be said to constitute the beginning of what people call philosophy. It is a faint recognition, though impalpable, indistinct, and not always conscious, of the presence of a value, a state of life, a condition of living, which is different from the one in which one is situated. A dissatisfaction of some sort subtly felt from within, though not clearly expressed consciously, is the incentive behind every effort, every activity, every enterprise, anything that man does in any way. If everything is all right, there would be no incentive to work. Something is wrong somewhere, and something has to be done about it. This necessity felt from within man, to do something, because something is not well, is the seed of philosophy that man sows in his life.

The Dissatisfaction of Man

No one in the world can be said to be fully satisfied with things. In whatever condition one may be placed, there is a kind of dissatisfaction. Nothing is complete in life anywhere. There are some complaints to make against everything. Nothing can satisfy anybody. The reason why, cannot be easily understood, though. One is likely to imagine that all the difficulties are socially constructed. Man looks around and sees people, and is thoroughly dissatisfied with the way in which they are behaving. "What a wretched society it is!"—often he complains under the impression that society is the source of the evil that he sees in life. He believes his sorrows are caused by other people. It is the cussedness of man's nature that is the source of his sorrows. Man is not behaving as man. "What man has made of man," says the poet. Society is not directing itself in the way it ought to. There is something dead wrong in the structure of human society. So, one looks up to the skies and exclaims, "What can I do?"

Government as a Solution to Man's Problems

Historians and students of political science tell us that originally people lived in a natural state. There was no society at all. There were only individuals scattered helter-skelter. There can be no organisation among people when they are in such a state of nature. This means that there was no regulation of any kind once upon a time. This appears to be a state of absolute freedom; Utopia indeed! But no. Historians, especially the philosophers of political science, tell us that this was a time when human beings lived like animals, and what law operated or prevailed at that time, cannot be easily known at present. There was insecurity prevailing everywhere on account of the impossibility of discovering the attitude of another in regard to oneself. If we do not know what others are thinking about us, or what the other is trying to do in respect of us, the problem is obvious. When man cannot know his future, he is in a state of insecurity; he is restless inwardly.

The discovery that historians of political science have made is that man invented a mechanism called government to free himself from this sense of insecurity, which was rampant in a state of affairs, where individuals had no rule or law among themselves. This is called the Social Contract Theory in politics. Man has manufactured a system of regulations, rules, etc., which he called government. People themselves have created it. They sat together, discussed among themselves as to what would be the best method according to which they should conduct themselves in society, and they thought there should be an agreement among themselves. This agreement among the people is called the law of the government. They imagined that they would then be secure and no trouble will come to them afterwards from any source, if there was a law which prevented them from being subjected to the onslaughts of uncanny forces and to the discomfort of an unknown future

But man was not satisfied. We have governments, but we are still crying, weeping, cursing, and worrying within ourselves that things are as bad as they were, and are, perhaps, even worse. This mechanism, this structure of governmental control or regulation, has not helped man in freeing himself from sorrow, which was there at the origin of things, and which is there even now. In some other form, may be, but it is still appearing and showing its face. It has taken a different contour, but it is still there. Man is the same old man, worrying as he was worrying many centuries back. He has the same problems.

Ethics as a Solution to Man's Problems

There is the science of Ethics, often called morality, on which people hang very much for a safe conduct of human life. This is another of man's attempts at trying to tackle his feeling of inadequacy, insecurity, and bondage. A standard or a norm is framed for the behaviour of people, and, if the norm is broken, that behaviour is called unethical, immoral, and so on. Thus, the religions of the world today, especially those which have leant too much on these norms of ethics and morality, have turned out to be nothing but mechanisms of do's and don'ts, a different set of mandates that compel men to behave in a particular manner. While man is forced to behave in a particular manner only, willy-nilly, by the regulations of the government, the mandates of ethics and morality compel him in another way and force him to behave in a standardised manner, whether he wants it or not. So, again, he is in a state of bondage. Not even a ray of freedom can be seen in life. There are always compulsions from every side. Religion compels everyone to say, do, and think in this manner or that manner; society forces in its own way; and so do political governments.

Basic Urge of Man Is for Freedom, not Bondage

It appears that man is a bound soul pressed into a concentration camp, and it further appears that he just cannot hope to discover what he is internally aspiring for. The world does not seem to have the capacity to deliver the goods. There is no freedom in this world. It cannot be seen anywhere. Everybody is tied down by the shackles of some system, regulation, law, ethics, morality,—whatever they may be.

Governmental laws are external mandates which force man to behave in a given manner. But man cannot be forced like that. Nobody wishes to be compelled to do, or even to think, something by force. There is a spontaneity in man. Every single individual asks for freedom and not bondage, be it of any kind whatsoever. Even to be subjected to the law of a government is a bondage, and to think what man aspired for was freedom! So, when men asked for freedom, they got bondage! From one kind of bondage they have entered into another kind; in the bargain, no freedom has come. Man, now, has a fear of a different type. While he was afraid of one individual or one group of individuals then, now he is afraid of a larger spectre that is before him, which he has himself created, and he does not seem to be any the better for it. The problem of man is inside man only. This is a very strange feature that thoughtful analysis of the human situation reveals. Adepts in this field have tried their very best to go deep into this tangle.

How is it that man is asking and searching for a thing which he cannot find in life? This again is a mystery. If freedom were unknown in this world, and if everybody were bound in some way or the other, or by something, it would be futile to seek it here. But man seeks nothing other than that. Is this not an irony? Is this not a contradiction? What can be a greater irony in life than to seek a thing in a place where it is not to be found? The human mind has tried its best to probe into these difficulties, and has invented various systems of living by which it may attain this freedom.

These daily activities of man, from morning to evening, are nothing but his attempts to achieve freedom. He is restless for one reason or the other, and the struggle to obviate the causes of restlessness takes the form of activity. Man is experimenting with the various phases of life by what is called activity, duty, and the like. Anything that he does, in any way whatsoever, is an expression of the energy within trying to break its bounds. But he has never succeeded in breaking through them. He has spent all his life in experimenting with things but has achieved nothing. So, a state of despair and a dissatisfaction with everything is the result. Then he sits quiet looking up, thinking that it is all a hopeless affair. Often people have to come to the conclusion that life is just not worth living. One does not see any meaning or any significance in anything, anywhere. Everything seems stupid; everything is nonsense! This is the first vision of life that one has before him. And, it is said that it is a good sign. It is an indication that the eyes are opening. Dissatisfaction with the first view of things is supposed to be the mother of all philosophies. When man casts an eye around, things do not satisfy him. It is in fact dangerous to be satisfied immediately, because things are alluring, tantalising, and facts are well camouflaged. If a camouflage or a make-belief can satisfy one, it is a sign of danger, because, 'things are not what they seem'. They are something, and they behave in a different way. The word "they" that is used here applies to everything, human and non-human. No person is what he appears outside, and no thing in the world is what it appears externally. Everything is different on the outside to the perception, to the vision. But man cannot easily believe that his knowledge is superficial only. That is why he is caught from every side.

Problems of Man

What are man's problems? What does he lack finally? It is an ocean of problems, and no one can easily give an answer offhand indicating the source of these difficuities. Man is apparently buffeted from every side. Man has problems within his ownself; problems from outside society; and problems and unknown difficulties descending from the heavens like natural cataclysms, catastrophes, etc. In Indian philosophical terminology, these difficulties arising from the three sources are called *tapatraya*, a problem which is threefold in its nature. Inwardly there is some problem, outwardly there is some, and from above there is something else altogether.

The fear that man has from things outside him, from men and things etc., is the external problem. One cannot trust things fully. There is an anxiety about everything. This is the difficulty that he faces from the phenomena outside.

There are also fears of a different type whose causes are unknown, which are capable of descending on man from above,—like floods, droughts, earthquakes, cyclones, tempests and thunderstorms, and other such natural calamities.

But over and above these, there are inward difficulties of one's own. Man is a psychological derelict in himself. There is a conflict in his own personality. Nobody can be sure even of his own self, what to speak of other people. We may not be able to trust others fully, but can we even trust our own selves! We cannot say what we will think the next day. Something seems to be working like a machine from inside us, and we seem to be untrustworthy to our own selves. Perhaps, this is the greatest danger in life about which one has to exercise a greater concern than in respect of other things.

The difficulties that man has to face from outside and from above, are not so acute as the ones that he has to face from within his own self. There are layers of man's internal personality which are at war with one another. Psychological problems are the greatest problems of life. The political, the social, and the economic problems etc. are but secondary compared to these psychological ones. The greatest difficulty is psychological. Man lives or dies only by his mind.

There are students of life who contend that the difficulties of human life are not outside in the political field, the aesthetic field, the moral or the ethical field, but are ingrained in the structure of man. These people are the psychologists or the psycho-analysts. According to them, it is futile to study things which are external as they are not the sources of human difficulties. Man himself is the source of his own problems. The source of man's sorrow is a lack of inward adaptation. The study of the individual has been recognised as something which is precedent or antecedent to social studies or the studies which are called the humanities. The study of man is the primary study, not the study of society or nature outside, because there is no society without the individual, and Nature as such is not the source of the problems.

Futility of Man's Attempts

Thus, the cultures and the civilisations of nations are studied with a hope of finding a solution to human problems. Students of history have busied themselves in such themes as anthropology and the descent of man from his origin. Various civilisations have been probed into, only with one intention; to come to some sort of a conclusion about man's present difficulties. People have studied various types of political governmental systems and evolved numerous methods of self-government. These have ended in nothing substantial, finally. The ethical sciences and moral codes have not really helped anyone. Many a time the discerning mind is inclined to believe that they are but man-made shackles. The norms of goodness and morality have not actually satisfied the soul of man. They have become annoying sources of a new type of bondage. People have taken to aesthetics, painting, drawing, music, literature, architecture, sculpture, and what not, with a view to find an avenue of escape from the turmoil of life as a whole, and these then become the vocations they are pursuing.

All these things have satisfied none. Man is, today, individually and personally, no better off than his ancestors as a human being. The various forms in which man's external pursuits present themselves, aesthetics, axiology (the study of the values of life), ethics and morality, sociology, civics, economics, political science, history, civilization and culture, which go by the name of "the humanities," all these are studied by people, who think that they can probe deep into the mystery of things but nothing has been found yet. They have only dug up thorns and pebbles, but not the gold or the treasures that they expected there. People are disappointed. They have struggled and struggled, and found nothing. Thus having come to no conclusion whatsoever in finding an answer, they lament, "We are helpless. We can say nothing except that we are helpless."

Here is a step taken as an advance in the field of philosophical analysis. The recognition of the total helplessness of the human individual is a sign of wisdom. The pride of man has to subside. The ego which struts around as an all-knowing entity begins to feel the pulse within. That is the beginning of true philosophy. When people refer to philosophical studies in their conversations, it may give the impression that they are thinking of some intricate academic matters. It is nothing of the kind. On the contrary, philosophy is a state of mind in which one finds oneself perpetually. Everyone is a philosopher in the sense that everyone recognises the indistinct presence and beckoning of 'a something'. That something is felt as a presence by a faculty which is not the eyes nor the ears nor any other sense organ, but a superior principle present in everyone. That superior light is the faculty of supernormal recognition.

Chapter II

WHAT IS PHILOSOPHY?

Philosophical Analysis Is Like Medical Diagnosis

Philosophical investigation can be compared, in a way, to medical diagnosis and investigation. It is a subtle and indepth understanding of the basic components of experience, similar to the investigation of various methods of medical application, as in the case of a chronic illness. Inasmuch as the organism of the body is internally related, the parts are connected to one another in an inseparable manner. Hence, when a part is investigated into, its relevance to the other parts cannot be ignored. Medical examination is a difficult subject. When a particular part of the body or an organ is ill, a good physician may have to understand the causative factors embedded in the whole system, and not merely in that particular organ. When a person is ill, even if it is by a mere cold, the whole body is ill, not merely the nostrils, or the nose. The illness is expressed or manifested through a particular channel, but the disturbance is in the entire organism. Likewise is human experience. Human problems do not come merely from one side, just as one is not ill only in one part of the body, though it may appear that he has only a sore in the foot, or a cold in the nose, or an ache in the head.

Thus, one may attribute the cause of his difficulties to certain factors of life. As mentioned earlier, man, mostly, attributes the causes of his experiences to social factors. This is an inadequate understanding of the situation. The outermost and the immediate phenomenon that man generally confronts in his life, is society, though the world is not made up merely of society. Nevertheless, he seems to be concerned only with that on account of a feeling that he is primarily involved in human affairs, and other things in the world are secondary, a notion that enters into his mind for obvious reasons. We are human beings, and, so, it is natural for our mind to assess things in a human manner. Cows go with cows; buffaloes go with buffaloes; frogs go with frogs; men go with men. They cannot go with anything else. This is a biological instinct that is at the root of man's reactions. Thus, man's philosophy becomes a human philosophy, and his efforts seem to be directed to human ends, and there is nothing else that can occur to his mind. But, to bring the analysis of medical examination once again, a mere human approach is not a proper scientific approach. The physician does not approach a patient as a father or a friend, but as a scientific impersonality, who wishes to *understand* and not merely emotionally *react*. Oftentimes people's experiences are emotionally stimulated. They are stirred up in some measure in their emotions, when they wake up in the morning and meet their friends. Their confrontation with their friends and their enemies is emotional rather than intellectual, rational, or philosophical. People are suddenly roused up into a feeling of satisfaction, or are plunged into a mood of melancholy or depression, which even though stimulated by non-human factors, seems to pass over from human beings. Though natural and important causes may be behind man's difficulties, like a wind that blows, or a flood that occurs in a river, or an earthquake that shakes him, man interprets them and tries to understand their relationship to him in terms of human beings.

A philosopher is not expected merely to think as a man or a human individual. The beginning of philosophy is the struggle of the mind to rise above the mere human perspectives. A difficult thing it is to become a philosopher! It is not merely reading a book, or going through the range of the history of the thoughts of philosophers. *One can become a professor of philosophy, but not easily a philosopher*. A philosopher is one who has an insight into the substantiality of things, and not the appearances they put on in their mutual relationship.

Philosophy Studies Even Notions

A philosopher must be able to stretch his mind beyond what merely appears to the eyes, into the field of what is not substantial and tangible, even if it may be of notions or concepts. Most of the matters that are important to man are mere concepts. Without these concepts and notions, he cannot live. They are necessary notions. For example human society is a phenomenon that can be cited. Really, there is no such thing as society. It does not exist. What is there, is only a heap of individuals. There are men and women and children. Nothing else is seen. Society cannot be touched. It cannot be even seen with the eyes. A society is a psychological interpretation of relational circumstance, so that it becomes a *relation* and not a *substance.* So are administrations, governments, etc. They are not visible to the eyes. Only people can be seen. The building bricks of administrative organisations, even of the human society for that matter, are the individuals which are the substances. So, when an attempt is made to define the content of philosophy, one would be landed in the definition of a substance, an existent something, rather than a notion. A distinction has to be made between a substance and a notion. An obvious example of this difference, as seen above, is the human society, which should be regarded as a notion, though a necessary notion. Every organisation, every institution is a notion. It is an idea which has been projected by a group of people for practical convenience in day-to-day existence. But, substantially, only people exist and not relations. What are relations then? The relations are psychological.

When a body, an organisation, or an institution, is to be formed, or a system of action is to be set up, minds join together, and act and react in a particular manner. This psychological action and reaction in a requisite manner, is the organisation, and, if this action and reaction ceases psychologically, there is, once again, a discrete, isolated phenomenon of individuals, existing without any society. If there were no mental reactions in human beings, they would remain as mere substances, isolated individuals, and not form a society or anything of the sort. So, in a philosophical study, the basic substance is investigated into so that it becomes easy to know what reactions it sets up through the characteristics it possesses. Human substances, called individuals, set up human reactions, and, therefore, there are human institutions—whatever be the largeness of these institutions. From two persons becoming friends and enlarging this friendship into a family group, it can expand into a community of people and, further, into a national spirit or an international organisation, and so on. Yet, the principle is the same. Human minds act and react. Therefore, what is called a social set up, whatever be the extent or the dimension of it, is psychological and not physical.

Philosophy Studies Change

No human institution survives for eternity. All empires came and fell. No kingdom succeeded for eternity, and no institution can, because all institutions which are humanly organised, are conditioned by the evolutionary factors to which the minds of people are subject, and, as there is an advance in evolution, there is, naturally, a change in the set up of psychic actions and reactions. Therefore, human institutions cannot be perpetually established in the world. No family, no nation, no empire can stand for ever, because it is not permitted by the law of evolution, just as one cannot be a baby always, though one was a baby once upon a time. A baby becomes a mature person, and advances. The systems of organisation in the form of social institutions grow into maturity, and they become old like the individual, then they decay, and they perish. The law of growth and decay that is seen in the individual personality and things, operates even in institutions. This is so, because institutions are only manufactured goods psychologically projected by the characteristics of the individual, which are subject to this evolutionary process of growth, decay, and final extinction. The whole world seems to be subjected to this law of evolution. Nothing can stand in the same condition for ever.

Now, when one observes this phenomenon of change to which everything seems to be subject, including human individuals, one is dragged, perforce, into a need to investigate into that which changes. If there is change, something is changing. It is not that change itself is changing. Change is a process. It is a condition into which something is subjected, through which something passes. What is this something which is evolving, which changes, which is subject to transformation, which grows, decays, and, finally, becomes transformed into extinction? This is the way in which a philosophical mind works. It cannot be satisfied with a mere first vision of things. A credulous mind or a baby's intellect takes things for granted. A toy is a toy, and it cannot be anything else. It is something worthwhile for a baby. But to a mature mind, it is a useless tinsel, which has no value. The value of a thing changes on account of a new interpretation to which it is subject. So, while man's thinking is generally like that of children,—even for grown-ups a building is a building, a land is a land, a man and a woman are a man and a woman, everything is as it is seen by the eyes to the prosaic perception, a philosophical analysis is a capacity specially exercised by the mind to delve deep into the substantiality of things rather than the contour which experiences put on. Things are not what they seem to be, and nothing is what it appears to be. History, whether it is astronomical or social, is a proof of the impossibility to finally trust anything as it is made visible to the eyes.

Philosophy and Science

Philosophy is a study of causes behind events, or, rather, the causes of effects, or, to push it further, it may be said to be a study of the ultimate cause of things. This is the subject of philosophy. Why should there be anything at all, and why should it behave the way in which it behaves? It is often said that science is distinguished from philosophy in this that, while science can tell the 'how' of things, it cannot explain the 'why' of things. That is not its field. The 'why' of anything is investigated into by the study known as philosophy. Unless the question as to the 'why' of a thing is answered from within oneself, one cannot feel finally contented. There is a mystery hanging above our heads, and everything seems to be a mist before us. Why should anything conduct itself or behave in the way it does? Social philosophies of different types study the nature of human behaviour. The science of sociology, again, confines itself to the 'how' rather than the 'why' of human behaviour. "How do people conduct themselves, and how do they behave in human society?" it asks. But we have a different faculty within us which puts the question: "Why do these people behave in this manner?" We often say, "I do not know why people are behaving in that way." Philosophy studies everything that it sees, everything that it senses, and anything that it can think of in the mind. It puts the questions of 'how' and 'why' to everything, and anything;—to every blessed thing. Any object of experience is subjected to analysis of this kind to the very core, threadbare, and one tries to go deep into its very roots. Every experience, external or internal, is an object, or a subject, of study in philosophy. Philosophy is a comprehensive science, if at all we can call it a science. It is a science in the sense that it is a systematic study, a logical approach, and does not take things for granted. It proceeds from the visible to the invisible. We may say, it proceeds from the particular to the general. This is the inductive system in philosophical analysis. Or, sometimes they say, the method adopted is called the Socratic method—a questioning attitude, a question which questions the question itself, and does not take anything for granted until a satisfactory rational ground is discovered behind the causes of these questions, which constitute human life in its present form.

Thus a philosophical insight is an awakening of a new light from within, with whose aid one can illumine the dark corners of the earth, and endeavour to see things in their true colours, rather than be carried away by their chamelion-like shapes and presentations.

Philosophy is the vision of facts as they are, divested of the imagination by which circumstances in life are construed to be quite different from what they really are.

The history of philosophy gives a list of great thinkers who conducted such investigations. It is also necessary for us to cover the range of all the possible channels of approach to the essence of things, which philosophers call Reality.

Chapter III

THE STRUCTURE OF THE UNIVERSE

What Is Reality?

There are two aspects of experience,—the real and the unreal, and everything can be divided into two camps,—that which really is, and that which is an appearance. That which does not partake of the characteristics of reality is called appearance. One of the philosophers has defined reality as that which persists in the three periods of time, that which existed in the past, that which exists in the present, and that which shall exist in the future also, without any change. But, with our eyes, we have not seen any such thing. There is nothing in the world which will stand this kind of a test of indestructibility, unchangeability, and permanence.

All the same, the inherent instinctive feeling of man that there exists such a reality, along with the urge to find a solution to the human predicament, motivates the search for reality, which, quite naturally and understandably, starts with the analysis of the immediately available human experience, which is the world.

The World Is Mechanistic in Nature

There is only the material world seen, and generally this is regarded as the reality. The world is the reality before man,—the physical world of the five elements: earth, water, fire, air and ether. The philosophical and scientific minds analyse this fivefold elemental existence into several bits of components, which may be called chemical compounds. There was a time when it occurred to the minds of thinkers that the whole world of physical matter was constituted of certain basic elements. These elements constituted every bit of matter, whatever be the way in which matter expressed itself,—it may be gold; it may be silver; it may be iron; it may be brick; or it may be a living body,—that made no difference. All these are material in their nature, and they are basically constituted of certain chemical stuffs. The analysis went ahead through the passage of various centuries, and as the scientists approached closer, the basic substance began to recede from their perception. Every time it looked different; never could it be grasped by their hands. The molecules appeared like atoms, and the atoms looked like electrical charges. But, whatever be the name that they gave to the nature of the discovery that was made through scientific observation, there appeared to be something outside their ken, a stuff, or a substance, or a 'thing-in-itself', whose nature was not easy to describe in language.

The world, or the universe, under this definition of being constituted of basic physical molecules, was defined as mechanistic in its nature. A mechanism is a system of operation where the parts are mathematically connected to other parts, and their mutual operation in collaboration also is mathematically constituted. A huge robot, or any other kind of industrial mechanism, is an example before us. We can precisely say how the machine works by a study of its parts. The whole can be studied by a study of the parts. This led to materialist science, and behaviourist psychology.

Even the modern allopathic science of medicine is based on this mechanistic notion of the structure of the human body. Its protagonists regard the human body as a kind of machine, whose parts could be studied as the parts of a motor car are studied. Each part can be pulled apart, and nothing happens to the other parts. One part can be repaired, fitted into that structure, and the machine is complete. It appeared that they could pull out parts of the body without affecting the whole system, because a mechanistic conception of the universe takes its stand on the principle that the whole is not different from the parts. The whole is only a name that is given to the assemblage of parts. But, is it true? A question is raised by the mind itself. Is man merely an assemblage of parts? Can a human being be created by putting together some legs, noses, eyes, and ears? Is it true that nothing happens to the human being when the limbs are severed and scattered in different directions?

The mechanistic notion of the universe was confirmed scientifically and mathematically many years back by such thinkers as Newton and his follower Laplace, who thought that the whole astronomical universe is capable of interpretation, almost like the working of a clock,—and everyone knows how a clock works. It has no life, yet it works. So, the whole universal action is a lifeless action, and bodily action is similar to that. If it appears that human beings have life, it is only an epiphenomenon, an exudation, a projection, a sort of appearance including even the intelligence and the mind; so they believed.

The Presence of Consciousness Needs Explanation

The behaviourist psychology, which is based on materialist science, holds the opinion that the mechanism of the body determines even the thoughts of the mind. This point may be considered from a purely logical angle of vision. There is what is called intelligence, which is an exudation of the body, a secretion of the brain, or a kind of phenomenon that is projected by the collocation of material forces. Well, it may be taken for granted that it is so. But, the fallacy is very easily discovered in this argument. No one will agree that his intelligence is the same as his body. Such instances as appreciation of beauty, or an adoption of an ethical conduct, etc. may be taken as commonplace examples of life. "This is beautiful": no one can say that his leg is making this remark, nor that his nose is admiring the beauty of an object, nor that even the limbs of the body put together are making this assertion. "This is a good gentleman"; "He is a highly moral individual": such statements as these do not seem to apply to the body, or the fingers, or the arms, or the tummy, or the back, or the bones, or the flesh, 'or the marrow of the individual. The morality of an individual, for instance, cannot be said to be the morality of the flesh, or the muscles, or the sinews. These ideas of values in life get abolished totally when the body or the material aspect alone is emphasised, and, worse than that, a difficulty arises of relating consciousness to matter.

Here is a serious logical problem. The relationship between two things has to be explained; here, the problem is of the relation between matter and consciousness. It is held under mechanised observations that intelligence proceeds from, or is exuded by, matter. This assertion would imply that the effect, which is intelligence, is already present in the cause, which is matter, because there cannot be an effect without a cause. Intelligence that proceeds from matter, consciousness that is the effect of matter, has to be present in matter which is the cause. If it is present, a question may arise, "which part of matter is occupied by consciousness ?" Matter is everywhere. The whole universe is matter, and nothing but . that. Can it be said that some point of space or a locality of matter is intelligent, or is the whole of matter intelligent? No one can say that it is located in one place or only in a little area of matter, because matter is an indivisible substance which is spread throughout space. Infinity is the name of matter. Thus, if the effect, which is consciousness or intelligence, is to be embedded in the cause, which is matter, it has to be present everywhere.

This conclusion is amazing and startling. It needs a logical and systematic re-analysis. Matter is the cause of intelligence: that is the thesis. But matter is everywhere. Therefore, the effect, which is intelligence, also, has to be everywhere, wherever matter is. Thus, the first acceptance that one is forced into is the conclusion that consciousness is everywhere, and it cannot be in one place only, because it is granted that it is an effect of matter, and matter is everywhere. This implies matter and consciousness are everywhere simultaneously. How can this be possible? Even if this position is accepted, another difficulty arises, which is not easily solved; viz., the relationship between effect and cause. The material scientists have not considered these difficulties properly. They have jumped suddenly into a hasty conclusion. The difficulties are apparent.

The relationship between cause and effect is a difficult thing to understand. There can be an identity or a difference between two things. A can be the same as B. or A is not the same as B. There cannot be a third relationship between two things. If A is the same as B, it is useless to call it A; unnecessarily another name is given to it. But if A is not B, it has no connection with B. Hence, it bears no relation to it. Therefore, it cannot be an effect of the cause.

Consciousness cannot be an effect of matter if it does not bear any relationship to matter. Thus, the relationship, if it obtains at all, has to be one of identity or difference. If it is identical, materialism falls in one second. The whole matter which is the universe would be aglow with consciousness. But if it is different, it does not follow that consciousness is exuded by matter. It stands as a separate identity.

Materialism is a monistic philosophy. It is not a dualistic doctrine. It does not permit the existence of consciousness outside matter. The monistic attitude of the materialist fails on account of his inability to explain the relationship of consciousness to matter. He is faced with twin choices so as to stick to his monistic stand. He must accept that matter and consciousness are identical. For this, he is not prepared. Then, he must deny totally the existence of consciousness. This, again, he cannot do, because the argument of the materialist is not the argument of matter; it is not matter that is speaking, it is consciousness that is holding an opinion. So, he is forced to accept the presence of consciousness. But, then, its relationship to matter remains unexplained.

Samkhya, or Dualistic Philosophy

The monistic materialism of utter materiality, lands us in a dualistic concept of matter and consciousness. The *Samkhya* philosophy also propounds the same theme. They maintain consciousness as a separate self-identical principle, —a distinct being, *Purusha,* as they call it. It has no connection with *Prakriti* which is matter. People felt a difficulty of their own in identifying consciousness with matter. So they created a philosophy of their own called *Samkhya* —"I cannot be the same as the body, and the body cannot be the same as me; consciousness is not matter, matter is not consciousness; yet both exist; I can see the body, and I can see that I have intelligence, also. So, intelligence is different from matter; *Purusha* is different from *Prakriti.*"

This may be considered as an advance. When two parties cannot reconcile themselves with each other in any way whatsoever, they say, "You mind your business, I mind my business." So, *Purusha* tells *Prakriti,* and *Prakriti* tells *Purusha,* "We mind our own businesses; we have no connection with each other; otherwise, we will come in conflict with each other, every day." Matter and consciousness fight with each other, but they would not want to continue this fight for ever. So, *Samkhya* came to make a truce of this war, and declared, "Peace, and no fight hereafter. *Purusha* is *Purusha; Prakriti* is *Prakriti.* Let them have their own positions, and have no connection with each other."

But this is a difficult thing, again. Two enemies are always enemies, even if they do not speak to each other. They will bear a grudge for ever. And, this system of duality, utterly isolating one camp from another, will not last for a long time. A difficulty arose, the truce was broken, and the two opponents would not occupy their own positions like that. *Prakriti* would not occupy its own position independent of *Purusha,* nor *Purusha* would exist independent of *Prakriti.* They clashed with each other. So, from one difficulty arose another difficulty. A problem cannot be solved by the introduction of another problem. But this is what has happened. The utter materialism of the monistic attitude to matter failed on account of the difficulty in explaining the position of consciousness in the universe. *Samkhya,* though it appeared as a solution, ended in nothing, like the formation of the League of Nations in days gone by, which did nothing, and ended in nothing finally. For the time being, it appeared that everything was in peace. But, that peace was broken by the confrontation of *Purusha* with *Prakriti,* and *Prakriti* with *Purusha.* They created a new genie, a kind of a goblin, as it were; viz., the individual *Jiva,* as they called, the mixture of *Purusha* and *Prakriti;* a little of consciousness and a little of matter, by an imaginary relationship brought about between the two principles.

The Doctrine of Samkhya Is basically not Different from Materialism

Samkhya is only a restatement of the same problem of the materialists. It is not a solution of the problem. They have only varnished the problem and put a little gild outside. But, inside, there is this iron core of the very same problem of materiality. It is surprising where the *Samkhya* has landed man. It has covered him, blindfolded him, made him a fool, as it were, and compelled him to think that everything is fine, while things are as bad as they were. Nothing is all right, everything has been in the same condition. The problem in the concept of materiality is the relationship between matter and consciousness. Now the relationship between *Purusha* and *Prakriti* needs explanation. What is the use of giving different names? The problem is the same. Previously what is called matter, is now called *Prakriti;* and what is earlier called consciousness is now called *Purusha.* A difference in terminology is not a solution to the problem. So, the doctrine of *Samkhya is* nothing but a materialistic doctrine itself, which has been reshaped by a camouflage of a so-called spirituality of *Purusha;* even as the materialistic science and philosophy conceded the existence of consciousness, but could not keep it aside, away from matter, nor could it bring it into the camp or the bosom of matter itself.

What is the relationship between *Purusha* and *Prakriti?* There is no relationship absolutely. There cannot be any relationship, because they are two utterly different elements. If they are utterly different, how does one know that they are different? Who tells that they are different things? Does *Purusha* say this, or does *Prakriti* say this? Who is making this statement that *Purusha* is different from *Prakriti?* It cannot be said that *Prakriti* is making this statement, because it is unconscious; nor can it be said that *Purusha* is making this statement, because it has no connection with *Prakriti*. It cannot even know that *Prakriti* exists. But, if it knows that *Prakriti* exists, it has established a relationship already; its independence has failed. And, if the establishment of relationship has taken place, the nature of this relationship between the two has to be explained,—a difficulty which was initially envisaged in understanding or studying the materialistic philosophy. How difficult things are! The solution does not seem to be anywhere in sight.

Patanjali's Proposition

Well, there were geniuses who thought they solved this problem by the introduction of a cementing link between the two. This is what Patanjali has done, for instance, in his *Yoga Sutras,* though in his novel way. The Yoga of *Patanjali* is based on the metaphysics of *Samkhya,* but it differs from *Samkhya* in one important point. It was realised that it was not possible to get on with these two utterly different principles *Purusha* and *Prakriti*. The difficulty is obvious, as was mentioned. How could anyone think of these two things, unless there is a thinker of the two things? The person, the element, or the principle, that is aware of the existence of *Prakriti* on this side, and *Purusha* on the other, remains as a third thing altogether. Such a witnessing principle cannot belong to either *Purusha,* or to *Prakriti*. But the *Samkhya* says that there cannot be a third thing. For it, there are only two things. The *Samkhya* defeats itself by positing two utterly different principles.

The metaphysical aspect of *Yoga* as propounded by Patanjali, felt the difficulty, and, so, there was an introduction of a deity called *Isvara*, in the Yoga philosophy. This word, *Isvara*, should not be associated with any devotional systems, or the God of the religions. Patanjali's *Isvara* is quite a different thing altogether. It is a pure '*deus ex machina*', a contrivance that has been made necessary to explain the relationship between one thing and another. Patanjali had his own arguments for positing the existence of *Isvara*. It was felt that there cannot be only two parties in a case. If there are two camps opposing each other, who will decide the case? People do good, people do bad. There is a reaction set up to every action, good or bad. Now, who will dispense justice in the form of a nemesis that is set up by actions, good or bad? A client cannot be a judiciary. It cannot be *Purusha;* it cannot be *Prakriti.* There is a third element necessary, a judge in a court. This judge was introduced by Patanjali, and he called this judge *Isvara.*

Who willed originally, who laid down this law that one body of matter should pull another body of matter in a particular manner? Why should there be this law of gravitation at all? If *Prakriti* can be independent of *Purusha* and *vice versa,* one body of matter can also be independent of another body. Everything can be independent of, or different from, everything else. Why not? What is the difficulty? But, that does not seem to be the case. There is mutual action and reaction seen among bodies. It is called gravitation in the physical field, and something else in the social and psychological realms. This cannot be explained unless there is a third element which is the causative factor behind the two parties which sets up action on the one side, and reaction on the other side. One part sets up action, another part sets up reaction. There must be a connection between the two. Otherwise, there is no reaction of action. This is a fact that is observed in life. So, the third principle is called *Isvara,* in the language of the Yoga of Patanjali. We may call this central judiciary in the cosmos, by any name we like.

This seems to be a tentative solution, but we will find that Patanjali has landed us in a problem again. It must be noted that the greatest problem of philosophy, is the problem of 'relation'. If this cannot be explained, nothing is explained in life. Instead of solving the difficulty of explaining the relation between two things, Patanjali seems to create another problem of a need to find a relation between three things,—*Prakriti, Pursha* and *Isvara.* How are they related to each other? Are they identical, or different? Now, again, the problem of identity and difference arises.

Philosophy seems to have failed. The analysis of the world leads us nowhere. The problems remain as problems, unanswered. Not a single question has been answered satisfactorily. That is where one stands, after a little bit of preliminary thought philosophically.

Chapter IV

THE STUDY OF THE SELF:
FROM PHYSICS TO METAPHYSICS

Nobody can deny the existence of human society, without which day-to-day life itself is unimaginable. The universe is made more of unseen, invisible things than what one can even conceive of. It is not merely what appears to be there to the eyes. There is a mystery behind it to be unravelled. The pure materialists and even the *Samkhya* thinkers, however, ignore this invisible but vital factors. Thus, they fail, finally. Not only this; probably, the very approach and the stance taken by them is inadequate to the purpose. Their failure to arrive at any satisfactory conclusion in the study of the universe from a purely materialistic and mechanistic point of view suggests that an entirely new angle of vision is called for.

Gravitation Suggests an Organic Interconnectedness in the Universe

Generally, we have the feeling that matter is contained as a substance inside space. Very rarely does one feel that there is such a thing called time. Man is inviolably connected with the process of time. Yet, he thinks very little of it, but is acutely conscious of space. The dimensions of matter, which man identifies with the substances of the world, are due to the extensions of space. There is what is called distance, and that principle of distance is due to the existence of space. Man has an intuitional apperception of the characteristic of space, such that he does not bother much about its nature. He thinks that it is all clear. Everyone knows what space is,—it is a kind of emptiness, we think, which contains every blessed thing. This was the original eighteenth or nineteenth century conclusion of even physics, which led to the notion that the universe of astronomy is an arrangement of material bodies which were formed out of the galaxies, and which constituted the solar system, the earth, the planets, etc.

However, it is not evidently easy to accept that bodies are scattered independently in space, as if they have no connection whatsoever among themselves. It is not that one mountain is here, another there; or one tree is here, and another there; without any connection between the two. If they were independent, there would be no gravitation at all. But even such bodies as planets are subject to this force of gravitation; what to speak of other things. There is an attraction of bodies in a mechanistic manner, as is usually held, conditioned by a mathematical formula. But, really, can the relation be purely mechanistic? How is it possible that there is such a pull among bodies, if there is no internal organic relation among themselves? This is a point that has been unearthed recently in modern physics. The presence of a pull known as gravitation implies, and should imply, an inward, or rather an invisible organic relation between one body and another, notwithstanding that there is a distance of some light years between them. Look at the distance between the sun and the earth,—an unimaginable one. Yet the gravitational attraction of the solar orb is so intense that it can compel the planets to move round in their orbits,—the spatial emptiness that is between them, making no difference. It is, therefore, not true that space is emptiness because by emptiness or vacuum, generally, an absolute nothingness is meant. An absolute nothing cannot become a medium of movement of any force such as gravitation. There is a necessary movement of a connecting link in an invisible form so that gravitation becomes possible. How could the phenomenon of a total vacuum operating as a medium of action between bodies be explained? The principle of gravitation is a visible indication that matter is not located in one place. There is an organic interconnection between bodies. This is a deeper implication that comes to the surface, when an attempt is made to understand the nature of space, and the relationship that obtains among bodies.

An affinity among bodies is what is called gravitation. When this force operates among human beings, it is biopsychic affection. It can also be repulsion under certain circumstances. There is chemical affinity and also psychological affinity, all which seem to be working among human beings and even animals. It appears that Nature cannot manifest its purpose except by expressing the inner content of its constituents. In every movement of Nature, whether it is organic or inorganic, there seems to be a secret characteristic which reveals the interrelatedness of bodies.

Precise Working of Material Bodies: An Indication of Cosmic Intelligence

The deeper does one go into the world of matter, and the further does one move in the direction of space, the more is the insight one gains into the secret of the operation of Nature, the secret being an organic relation among bodies, which appears to be outwardly scattered in space. It is impossible humanly to imagine how the earth, for instance, can move along the same track which it was following for aeons up to this time, as if there is a set of rails laid down on its path in space. Man is used to thinking that things, like the planet earth, are inorganic, inanimate, incapable of thought, without eyes to see, and minds to think. But the precision with which bodies work surpasses even the best mathematical imagination. Perhaps, man has invented the system of mathematics only on the observation of the way in which material bodies operate. We are not intending to refute the opinion of rationalists, like Kant, however, in connection with the grounds of mathematical intuition. It cannot be explained how such a precision can be possible at all, where the action of the mind is not even apparent. Though this is difficult to understand because of man's habit of thinking, probably, finally, he will have to come round to attribute an intellect or a reason to what goes as inanimate existence. The inward affinity that physical bodies reveal in their activities would sound as an implication of an organisation that they form among themselves. There is, perhaps, a cosmic society, even as man has his own little, small human society.

The social sense that human beings have is a peculiar phenomenon. As observed earlier, the notion of human society is a psychic network, which operates invisibly and subtly, connecting bodies or individuals into a form of organisation called human society. In the formation of this organisation, the bodies do not actually collide with one another. There is no physical contact, necessarily. One human being can be several miles away from others. Yet they can form a body. This shows that the system of organisation or mutual relationship has little to do with spatial distance. It is something different altogether.

If society is nothing but an organisation of inward affinities, as is the case with human society, one can very well agree that there is no way of explaining the intricate features behind the operation of Nature except by accepting that there is a society of cosmic substances. Is not the solar system thought to be one organisation? Certainly, so. But the distance that is there between one planet and another, or between the planets and the sun, or, as the astronomers point out, between the sun and the other galactical bodies, is vast, enormous! It is said that there are stars whose presence cannot be known even with the most powerful of telescopes. But their presence exerts an influence of a unique nature by means of emanation of rays, which, today, is recognised as a vital living influence. Thus, the acceptance of the possibility of a cosmic society leads to the acceptance of an intelligence behind it, from the observed fact of the precise working of the bodies. Else, why should dead matter behave so sensibly and purposively?

Man does not seem to be living merely by the operation of physical objects which are visible to the eyes. Perhaps, he is even more dependent on invisible influences than on visible things, and his life seems to be connected to factors which range far beyond human perception and conception.

This is why, today, philosophers have stumbled, somehow, on the acceptance of a *process,* rather than a *location,* of bodies. Earlier, it was thought that things existed, or things can exist, only within the boundaries of their bodies, and that they cannot have any relevance beyond their location But, the concept of *process* melts down this boundary that is set to the bodies of substances, and *bodies seem to flow into one another* rather than maintain their isolated existences. There is always a craving within every body to become a part and parcel of another body. This is the principle of affection, the principle of love that is seen in Nature. It becomes more and more manifest as one rises to organic levels. This does not mean that it is absent in inorganic Nature, but merely that it is not visible to the naked eye.

Conclusions of Science: Man Is not Outside the Universe

What does the modern scientist say?

Matter has been dematerialised. Matter is no more considered to be a hard, solid substance. Man is gradually evaporating into thin air, so thin, so ethereal, and so fine that a time has come now when it is not possible to distinguish his own presence from the wider atmosphere of the universe. The observing scientist, or the philosopher, is inside the universe. This is important to remember. How can man look at the universe when he is a part of it? How can man study anything in this world? How can he make an analysis of any object, if he is not really outside it? From the fact of the conclusions that one arrives at through the consequences following from the law of gravitation, it follows that the universal structure cannot exclude the contents thereof. Man is not outside the universe. This should be a simple fact. If he is not outside the universe, how can he study the universe? Where comes the need, and the necessity, or even the possibility of his observing anything? Here is the crux of the whole situation. The problem that hangs like an iron curtain in front of the modern scientist is this difficulty of his inability to disentangle himself from the object of his observation. The great physicist, Heisenberg, discovered that he was involved in the very thing in which he was engaged. The body of the scientist is not outside the body that is to be observed. This is a kind of corollary that follows from the famous theory of Relativity. The space-time-gravitation cosmos is one complex, or it may be called a compound, if you like. It is such a terrific phenomenon that one gets frightened even by thinking of it.

Study of the Self Is Imperative to the Study of the Universe

While studying the non-mathematical, or, rather, the super-mathematical nature of subatomic structures,—this is the field of subatomic physics,—the nuclear physics which has been studied in quantum mechanics, and the theory of Relativity, noticed that the force of gravitation, which ruled the world of space and time, had to be reconciled with. This great task, Einstein took upon himself, when he was working at the theory called the Unified Field Theory, wherein "this" is identified with "that",—*tattvamasi*—"That thou art!"—the famous doctrine of the *Upanishad*. The quantum mechanics of Max Planck may be said to be the study of the "thou" or the "this", the nuclear element, or the visible object, which is immediately present as an individual structure; and the "that" is the space-time continuum and the gravitation of the universe, which Einstein studied in his General Theory of Relativity. The Special Theory and the General Theory put together, present a tremendous upheaval in the discovery of science. *Man is forced to study the universe together with a study of his own self, because he is not outside the universe.*

Inasmuch as man is not outside the universe, he is integral with it. He is a small universe in his own self. Whatever is in Nature should also be within him, and the system which is seen to operate within himself may be said to be the system that operates in external Nature also. So, Indian philosophers diverted the attention from the objective universe to the subjective individuality in order that *the whole cosmos could be envisaged at one stroke.*

There is an analogy in Indian logic called *"sthalipulaka nyaya,"* the argument of the recognition of the boiling of rice in a pot. While boiling rice in a pot, if it is required to know whether the rice is fully cooked or not, one grain is squeezed; if it is seen to have been cooked, well, it may be concluded that the whole rice has been cooked, and every grain need not be individually inspected.

So is this analogy of the study of the cosmos by a study of man, as such. The study of man is the study of the universe. "Know thyself" is the oracle of Delphi; *Tattvam*asi, is the proclamation of the *Upanishad.* That the knowledge of the self is the knowledge of the cosmos is a universally accepted doctrine of all philosophies and religions today.

Many a time, one is not able to understand how it is possible for one to know the universe when one is here as a separate individual. Where comes the connection between the knowledge of one's own self and the knowledge of the universe, or vice versa? The reason is simple. The universe is a complete organism, comparable to the human organism, so to say. A *complete organism is a total Selfhood. The whole cosmos is an organism,. and it is Selfhood in its nature.* Its Selfhood can be compared to one's own selfhood, because it is inseparable from one, and one is inseparable from it. That is how man can, perhaps, try to understand it. The study of the universe is the study of the Self of the universe, and the study of the Self of the universe cannot preclude the study of one's own self. The knowledge of the universe is the knowledge of the perceiver of the universe; i.e., one's own self. If one knows one's own self, well, everything else also is known simultaneously, because man is the symbol, or the microcosmic specimen of whatever constitutes Nature as a whole. One thing is the same as the other.

Perhaps, here, one gradually stumbles again, upon the truth that the knowledge of God and the knowledge of the Self, means the same thing. They are not two different things. God is the name that is given to the Self of the cosmos, the vitality behind everything, the indivisible compound and the utter reality of the most inexplicable character behind and within the universe. The knowledge of the Self is the key to the knowledge of anything.

All philosophy, or any kind of investigation for that matter, commences with immediately available evidence. This is the method followed by logic, where, from the particulars one goes to the generals; i.e., from available information the implications therefrom are dug deep into, or, the other way, from the basic indubitable fact of being, all else is derived as a corollary. The fault of the materialists lay in this that they misunderstood what the most immediate fact is. They took it to be the world that they see around. They ignored the most immediate thing, one's own existence. No one can doubt one's own invulnerable reality as the foundation for any thought or action.

Chapter V

THE NATURE OF THE INDIVIDUAL

The Initial Predicament

Human personality is not a granite or flint pillar. Man is not a solid object. "Your personality," or "my individuality,"—whatever it may be called,—is not a solid object like a stone, a brick, or a heavy substance. It is a movement, a continuous transition, rather than a thing that exists exclusively. Man is a concentrated point of movement. This is an important thing to remember. Movement can be higgledy-piggledy, chaotic action, running about in any direction, or like the cyclone or the wind that blows, but the movement that is human personality is not a jumble of agitation. It is not a tempest that blows in any direction as it wills. It is a well organised purposive movement. There is a system even in madness, as they usually say. In this transitoriness that the human personality is, in this movement that man is, in this complex of forces rather than of substances that he seems to be, there is an order, a system, a method, and a logic of its own. That is why human beings are actually sane and not wild sceneries: If man were to blow like wind, and the components of his personality were to go anywhere they willed, like a storm in the ocean, he would be torn to pieces; a part of him would be there, and another part of him would be anywhere else.

Does not everyone think that he has a status and a substance of his own, which makes him feel that there is a method in his existence? Everyone has a memory of the past, and an anticipation of the future. The memory of the past is an important aspect of human psychology, which brings us to the point of a consideration of there being a connection between the past and the present,—to mention only one aspect of it. If the past had no relationship with the present, there would be no such thing as memory. How could anyone know what happened to him days back, when he is now, today, many days afterwards? There is, in this transitoriness of the motion of the mind, a continuity that seems to maintain itself. If this continuity were not to be there, there would be only bits of thoughts, like bricks thrown here and there, without any kind of a cementing element in them. Every moment man thinks of one thing; and every other moment he thinks of another thing. There is not always a connection of one thought with another thought. Though it is true that there is a psychological disparity in the human personality, accepting and granting that there is a multiplicity of thoughts and feelings arising in minds every moment of time,—man keeps on changing his moods and feelings, thoughts and volitions all the time,—yet, there is a unity that is maintained by him, all the same.

There is a differentia of the selfhood present in every object. Everything regards itself as itself. "I am myself, you are yourself," says everyone. This so-called affirmation of a self-identity of any particular thing, is the 'selfhood' of that thing. It may be even an atom,—it maintains itself. There is a pattern of compactness, which even a small atom maintains. It cannot become something else. The affirmation of the compactness of a particular thing is the selfhood of that thing. So, everybody has an insistence or a persistent feeling of maintaining an indivisibility, or an isolation of oneself

This study has been taken up in the *Vedanta* philosophy. It asks: "What are you?" What is this personality that is referred to? What does man see when he looks at himself? He sees only the body, a six-foot height. Is this the self? It is taken for granted, generally, that the body is the self, because the "I" that everyone speaks of is generally associated with the body. This is a common feature among everyone. It can be easily observed in our own selves: we say, "I am tall; I am thin; I am heavy; I am light; I am strong."

Sometimes we say, "I am hungry; I am thirsty." When we say I am hungry, I am thirsty, we are speaking in a manner different from the way when we said that we are tall, short, etc. Or, sometimes, we say, "I am upset; I am unhappy, I am agitated; I am annoyed; I am disturbed." Here, statements of this kind, naturally, do not refer to the body. And, "I slept yesterday, I had a good sleep";—when we speak like this, we are referring to a different personality. An analysis of the structure or the components of the individuality of a person has resulted in a discovery of what man really is.

Sometimes we talk of ourselves as, "I am Mr. So-and-So, I am Mrs. So-and-So, I am a judge, I am a minister, I am a rich man," and so on. This is to define an individual by social relationships. When we say, "I am hungry, I am thirsty", we refer to ourselves in a manner different from the way when we talk of our height, weight, etc. When we say, "I am happy, I am upset, I am unhappy, I am agitated, I am annoyed, I am disturbed"; or when we talk of any individual as "intelligent, good, efficient, moral, ethical, rational," etc., an inward constitution is referred to and not the physical body. Again, when we say, "I slept yesterday, I had a good sleep," a different personality is indicated.

Thus, we refer to man at different levels of understanding, though it is another matter that, generally, there is a mix-up. These different levels may be termed as the layers of personality. Even the psychologists and psycho-analysts hold that man is but layers of psyche. He is not one mass of mind like a heap. Man is, again, layers vertically, like clouds which form themselves into a thick mass by the coming together of various strata of atmospheric pressure. The psyche seems to be a heap of clouds, but made up of different strata.

Human personality, thus, is said to be constituted of certain layers, which may be considered to be material, basically. The *Vedanta* philosophy accepts the fact of the existence of matter, though it has its own definition of it, quite different from that of *Samkhya* or the materialistic definition.

It was seen that society is but a notion. Does it exist? The existence of society cannot be denied. It is as real as human beings, or matter. If a thought or a notion has as much reality as matter, can it be considered to be constituted of a type of matter? Can the psyche be a substance? Yes, says Vedanta. This, probably, is one of the ways of understanding matter, as referring to the constituent substance of the layers of the human personality.

The body is a material substance, but constituted of layers of matter, and not one solid thing. All these different layers of personality may be brought under three broad categories: *Gross Body, Subtle Body* and *Causal Body.*

The Gross Body is the physical sheath; The Subtle Body is the psychic one. Though, when man consciously thinks, he cannot think of himself to be anything other than the physical body, but, mostly he is psychological in nature. Human life is more mental than physical. Actually, it is the essence of one's personality.

In passing, it should be mentioned that there is another familiar classification, which says that the human personality is made up of layers or *koshas,* namely: *annamaya kosha, pranamaya kosha, manomya kosha, vijnanamaya kosha,* and *anandamaya kosha.* But this classification is not different from what is given above. *Annamaya kosha* is the Gross Body, the next three *koshas, viz., pranamaya kosha, manomaya kosha,* and *vijnanamaya kosha,* constitute the Subtle Body, and the *anandamaya kosha* forms the Causal body.

Gross Body

The Gross Body, known as *sthula-sarira* in Sanskrit, is nothing but the physical body. This is the outermost layer. This mass of flesh, bone, marrow, and the solidity that is seen, is the physical body. It is called the *annamaya kosha.* In

Sanskrit, *anna* means food. It is said that the physical body exists and is maintained by the food and drink that one takes. If one does not take meals for days together, he gets emaciated physically. The physical matter, which is the physical body, is worn out on account of no plastering applied to the physical structure, just as walls, if they are not plastered, wither and fall. Everyday, one has to eat food. The energy that is present in the vitality of the food is the source of the strength that is gained by the physical body. The body is made up of the essential components of one's parents. A very subtle, minute, potentised form of the physical essentiality of the parents becomes the source of the physical body. So, matter is the origin of the body. It may be a highly potentised form like an homeopathic medicine. Nevertheless, it is physical. This little drop of a force, with which man originates his physical life, grows in thickness, solidity, substance, length, breadth, height, and weight, but after all, with all its features, it still remains a physical substance only,—a Gross Body.

The physical sheath is inert, essentially. Matter has no consciousness. Man can be insensible at times when the vitality of the body is withdrawn. There can be schizophrenic action by which the mind splits itself into parts, and one person imagines himself to be two, three, four, etc. In a paralytic stroke a part of the body loses consciousness or sensation. Paralysis is an outstanding example of one's having a physical body, and, yet, having no sensation about it, no consciousness of it. The body is not the same as consciousness. Many materialists, and schools of this kind, imagine that consciousness is an exudation of matter. This cannot be, because consciousness is that which is aware of the existence of the body and it cannot be an effect of that body itself, as it is prior to the body. The cause is there which is the knowing factor. How could the body, if it be the source of consciousness, be the object of the very knowledge which it produced from within itself? Consciousness cannot be identified with the body. This is made clear when it is seen in one's own life that existence as a conscious entity, even without being conscious of the body, is possible. One of the examples is the phenomenon of dream and sleep, in which states the body is present, but consciousness of it is absent; and man is not dead, he is alive. So, man can exist as a conscious entity, and a living being, even without connection with the physical body. This Gross Body, or the physical sheath, is, therefore, not the true personality of man.

Subtle Body

Inside the physical body there is the astral body, or the subtle body. It is more rarefied and ethereal than the physical one. In Sanskrit, it is called *sukshma-sarira.* Sometimes this *sukshma-sarira,* or the astral body, is also called *linga-sarira.* In Sanskrit, *linga* means an emblem, and insignia, a mark, or an indication. One may wonder why this Subtle Body is known as *linga,* or an indication, or a mark. It is because whatever the *sukshma-sarira, or* the Subtle Body is, that man is. It is an indication of what man is made of. The physical body, or the physical feature, or the physiognomy of the body, is also an expression of the internal composition of the Subtle Body. Electricity is there inside physical matter. Something like that, one may say, is the way in which the Subtle Body is inside the physical body. The Subtle Body is a force. It can be compared to electric energy to some extent. It is not a hard substance. This Subtle Body, or the *sukshma-sarira,* or the *linga-sarira,* is the essence of one's personality. All that one is, all that one thinks, contemplates, and conducts, is the outcome of the nature of this Subtle Body which is within. Just as the physical body is made up of the subtle essence of the food that the parents have taken, and also the food that one eats, the Subtle Body is constituted of many other small components. *Prana* is a part of the Subtle Body; senses are a part of the Subtle Body; mind is part of the Subtle Body; the intellect is part of the Subtle Body. These are broad divisions; further subdivisions can be made, if one likes, on deeper analysis.

What Is Meant by Prana?

What is meant by *Prana?* What is life? The biologists tell us that there is a thing called life which is incapable of identification with matter. Though, many times, mechanistic materialists have held the opinion that life is not different from matter, it has become very difficult to accept this doctrine. How can anyone say that life is the same as brick, or a body with which one is lumbering, and without which also one can exist? It is seen that man can exist even without being conscious of the body. If the body were the same as life, life would be extinct when it is dissociated from the body. But man is alive even in dream, sleep, and states of deep concentration. In deep meditation one is not aware of the body. Man would be dead at one stroke, if it were true that matter is life, in conditions when the body is not an object of his consciousness. It is not true that matter is the same as life. They are two different things. But it is difficult to understand what the relationship is between these two. No one has ever come to a final conclusion as to what life means. It is this life-force that is called *prana-sakti.*

There is the *prana-sakti,* the power of the *prana. Prana* is vitality, living force, organic energy. It is a living, protoplasmic organismic, and energising vitality in man.

Sometimes *prana* is identified with breath. But it is interior even to breath. The blacksmith applies a kind of pressure upon a bag called the bellows, and he pumps air into the fire to make it ignited. The air that is pumped is not the pressure itself. The two are different. The air that he pumps moves due to the pressure that he exerts. Something like that is the case with the relation between the breath that is outside and the energy that is inside. There is a pressure that is exerted upon the air that is breathed by inhalation and exhalation. The metabolic process of the physical body is conditioned by the *prana,* the movement of the vital energy within man. But, wherefrom has this pressure come? Who is this blacksmith that pushes the bellows in order that the air may be concentrated upon the fire that is to be ignited? This is another important question.

Source of Prana

The vital energy within man is the sum total of his strength. Whatever strength or energy that one has, is nothing but the *prana*. It does not always come just from the food that one eats. Though fuel is necessary to ignite fire, fuel is not the same as fire; petrol is not fire, though petrol is necessary for ignition. There is a difference between the heat, and that which causes the heat to ignite itself by means of a fuel action. So, while energy is accelerated, accentuated, and enhanced by consumption of food, it is not identical with strength itself. Strength is an impersonal capacity that is within man, the force that is inside. How does man gain strength at all? It is not merely from the almonds that he eats, or the milk that he drinks. A corpse also can have food thrust into it, milk may be poured into its mouth, but it cannot gain strength. Any food that is served to the corpse cannot infuse energy into it. Another principle, called vitality, is necessary for the energisation or the digestion of the food that is eaten. Vitality is that which helps the working of the medicine that is taken, but if the vitality is gone, medicine is dead matter. It helps no one. So is the case with food. Food is also a kind of medicine that is taken for the illness of hunger, but it itself cannot provide the energy, unless there is vitality within. Wherefrom does the vitality come?

Indian philosophy in its higher reaches opines that the energy of the individual comes from the cosmos. It does not arise merely from the food that is eaten. Sun is the source of energy; oxygen is the sourc of energy; the five elements outside are the sources of energy; the whole universe is a mass of energy. To the extent man is in union with the universe, in the proportion to which he is in alignment with the forces of Nature, in that proportion, and to that extent, he is strong. So, strength emanates from the cosmos; it does not come from any other mechanical activity like physical exercise and the meal that one consumes, though these are of course, accessories. Accessories are not to be identified with the primaries. This is important to remember.

The thoughts of the great thinkers in India rose up to the heights of a cosmic identification of all things. They would not interpret anything without relating it to the universe. The universe is the source of energy. It is the dynamo that generates the energy which is the source of the movement and life of everything.

Functions of Prana

The *prana* is a common name that is applied to the total capacity in man, the energy of the personality, but it performs different functions. When a man does the work of dispensing justice, he is called a judge; when he is a chief executive of a district, he is called a collector; when he dispenses medicine, he is called a physician; and so on. The same person is known by different names on account of the functions he performs. So is this *prana* which performs five functions. When one breathes out there is exhalation, and *prana* is operating. *Prana* is a term that is used in a double sense. It indicates the exhaling force, and also the total energy of the system. So, *prana* means two things, the force that expels the breath out in exhalation, as also the total energy. The force by which one breathes in is called *apana*. The force that circulates the blood through every artery, vein and every part of the body equally, is *vyana*. It is known that the body is connected to other parts in such a harmonious manner that if any part of the body is touched, the sensation is felt in every other part also. This sensation that is felt in every part, as a wholeness of one's personality, is due to the *vyana* operating, a particular aspect of the function of the energy, which moves throughout the body equally. The energy that digests the food is called *samana*. There is another force which causes the deglutition of food. When food is put into the mouth, it is pushed inside to the oesophagus, through the part of the throat by which food is swallowed. An energy operates here. If that energy does not work, the food will be sticking there; it would not go in. This is *udana,* which enables the food to move in. It has other functions also; it separates the body at the time of death, and it also makes one to go to sleep.

There are other minor functions of *prana* mentioned in Yoga scriptures. But it is sufficient to know that *prana, apana, vyana, samana* and *udana* are the five principal designations of a single energy,—not five different things—just as one person can perform five functions. All this structure is in the Subtle Body.

Harmonious Balance of Prana Is Necessary

These different aspects or forces of the *prana* must be kept aligned in a methodical manner, so that they flow through the nervous system as water flows through a pipe. When there is a clogging of the pipe, the water does not flow properly. If there are sand particles sticking, or if there is any dust or debris inside the water pipe, there is no flow in a smooth manner. When there is no fluent breathing, when there is heaving breath, there is irregular activity of the *prana.* The *prana* is a homogeneous energy that flows through the entire system of the person. It is not supposed to be concentrated in one place. If there is such concentration, one can have ache in that particular part of the body. When one walks too much for miles, there is felt ache in the legs, because all the *prana* has gone to the legs. If one thinks too much, there can be headache, the *prana* rises up to the brain in intense thinking and worrying. Whenever there is excessive activity in any part of the body, the *prana* flows through in that direction. It is noticed that one feels like sleeping after a heavy meal. The reason is that blood goes to the stomach for the purpose of the digestion of the food, and when the blood moves, the *prana* is drawn towards it. The brain then has less of *prana* at that time, and so one dozes. If one does not eat well, that day one does not sleep well.

Prana gets irregularly distributed in the personality on account of desires, primarily. Man is full of desires. No one is free from them. But, if they are wholesome desires, harmonious with the atmosphere or the environment in which one is, they do not cause agitation. There is nothing devilish about desires as such, but, then, there is nothing devilish about anything in the world, ultimately. Everything is right, provided it is in its allotted place. Only when a thing is put out of context, when it is misplaced, or is given an excessive importance, especially when there is intense love and intense hatred, the *prana* is thrown out of gear, and there is a lack of its equidistribution in the body.

Love, of course, is good, and man lives only by love;—certainly so. But it does not mean that one should pour one's love on a particular object only. The lowest kind of knowledge is that where there is concentration on a finite object, as if it is everything. Love is the source of our vitality, energy, health, and sustenance; but *love directed exclusively to a single object is a danger.* There, *prana* is directed unwholesomely in one direction only, cutting off its relationship with other objects.

Man's strength depends upon the energy of the cosmos. He derives his strength from the universe. So, if he is not harmoniously related to the totality of the atmosphere, which is the universe, but disharmoniously concentrates his love, or affection, or hatred towards a particular object, he is dissociating himself from the other parts of the universe. Thus, laying excessive emphasis on one part only, towards which the *prana* moves, the mind goes, and is in that object for the time being, and is wrested out of other parts of the universe. Then he is a friend of one thing, and an enemy of another. When there is love for any particular object, enmity, automatically, is created towards that object which is not loved. Though this is not usually called enmity, here is a psychological implication that one is not equally considerate towards the other aspects of Nature, because of the excessive consideration that is bestowed upon one object. And, here is the source of physical illness and mental frustration.

It is a mistake to think that things are gained by loves concentrated on objects. Here is a blunder in the understanding. Then, why does anyone love anything excessively? What is the purpose behind it? The purpose is simple,—a miscalculation of the processes of the mind. The mind calculates wrongly when it imagines that excessive love, when poured upon an object, is the source of satisfaction that it gains from that object. It is always imagined that joy comes from things outside, from objects of sense. This is not true. This fact must be kept in mind always. *Our* satisfactions are not the outcome of attachment to objects. On the other hand, joys are the result of harmony with things. The more is man in harmony with the world outside, equally, not with excessive pressure exerted upon any part, the more is he happy. But, if he exerts too much in the direction of a particular object,—it may be a human being, or an inanimate object; it may be wealth, it may be property, it may be a building; it may be even a social status, love of name, fame, power, authority,—even these are objects, if there is too much concentration on these, he dissociates himself from the harmonious relationship that he is expected to maintain with the whole atmosphere. All these things explain how *prana* can be wrongly distributed.

In the process called *pranayama,* one is asked to keep the different forces of *prana,* aligned in a methodical way. As one derives one's strength from the cosmos, one must try to unite oneself with the cosmic energy. This is not merely a closing of the nostrils and holding the breath, as votaries of *pranayama* sometimes may tell. *Pranayama* is not possible and should not be conducted if one is emotionally disturbed in any manner. It is a dangerous technique, if it is practised by a person who is not emotionally calm and mentally balanced. An unbalanced person should not do *pranayama,* and a person who is deeply worried over a heavy sorrow or is sinking in grief should not practise *pranayama. Pranayama* should not be practised after a heavy meal, because the *prana* is concentrated on the stomach at that time. Similarly, it should not be practised after a long walk of several miles. There are many such minor details concerning *pranayama*.

Prana Is the Connecting Link between Mind and Body

The connection between the mind and the body is *prana*. When a thought arises, immediately the *prana* vibrates, and it produces an impact upon the body. Any kind of thought that is generated in the mind, has its force communicated to the body. If one is upset in the mind, this mood of the mind is transmitted to the body immediately, and the liver goes off; there would be no hunger that day; one says, "No, today I don't eat! My son has died; my mother has gone; I have lost all my property; I am in a helpless condition; I have no hunger today, I cannot eat." What has happened to the hunger? The sorrow that has descended upon the mind has been communicated by the *prana,* as if by an electric wire and the liver, the stomach, and everything has gone out of order. If anyone is happy, he has a tremendous energy; and even if he has not eaten for four days he will say, "I shall lift bricks!" Man can lift a stone and carry a tree, even if he has not eaten for days, because he is happy for some reason. "Oh! I am so happy, I am full, complete, everything is fine, I can do any work that you give me." But if he is grieved, even if he has just eaten a heavy meal, he cannot get up from his place, let alone lift things. He needs someone else to lift him then. "I am drooping, please lift me," he will say. What power thoughts have! The mind communicates its impressions through the *prana* to the body, and the body is affected sympathetically. So, this is the relationship between the mind and the body through the *prana,* which is such a mysterious collection of forces.

Essence of Subtle Body Is a Totality of the Psychic Personality

It is observed on an analysis that man is constituted of subtle layers of personality within the physical body, and he is more a mind than a body. Though man looks like a body and it appears as if the body is everything, the truth is otherwise. Human life is more mental than physical. *The processes of the mind are the processes of human life, rather than the circumstances of the physical body.*

Prana is only one aspect of the Subtle Body. There are other more important and vital aspects of it, which are mentation, volition, feeling, intellection, etc. This so-called Subtle Body is a great wonder. A lack of sufficient knowledge of its structure is the reason why there are so many schools of thought concerning the theory of knowledge,—how knowledge arises in the mind at all. Centuries of discussion have passed, and even today the controversy is continuing. How does one know anything at all? Philosophers call this science, Epistemology. Is knowledge imported from outside and planted in one's heart so that one knows what things are outside, or is knowledge exported from inside? Where is the location of knowledge? Where is it rooted? From where does it rise? It must exist somewhere, in order that it may become manifest in the form of man's experiences. This is the reason why one has to go a little deep into the nature of the Subtle Body. It is subtle because it is superphysical, is incapable of grasp by the sense-organs. It cannot come under the grips of even ordinary thinking, because thinking itself is a part of the way in which it works. The Subtle Body is a totality of man's psychic personality. By Subtle Body is not meant merely the mind, or the intellect, or the emotion, etc. *It is the total of what man is made of.* It is the entire energy reservoir of oneself, or, *rather, it is oneself.* The individuality, the personality, or the so-called characteristics exhibited in one's daily life, are a procession of the stuff of which the Subtle Body is made.

The activities which are psychological are the movements of the Subtle Body. It operates in the dreaming state, and also in the waking state. It does not operate in the deep sleep state. The light of the psyche is flashed forth through the apparatus of the sense-organs, and that is why man is having sensory knowledge, perception of things outside. It is not the eyeballs that see, or the ear-drums that hear, but the energy that is pumped out with a great velocity from within that becomes responsible for the externalised intelligence, which is called perception, or knowledge of the world. One is urged forward with a tremendous strength which constitutes the Subtle Body. The word "body" is used here because there is no better word for it in the language. *Actually, it is not a solid substance. It is an energy-complex, an electromagnetic field; an energy centre, a pressure-point which pulsates with such a force that it never allows man any rest.* He is pushed out of his own self, as it were. He is compelled, as it were, to become something different from what he is. That is why man is so eager to see things outside, rather than to look within.

All the thoughts of the mind are concerned with things outside it, and the whole engagement of life, or, rather, the business of life, may be said to be man's concern with everything other than his own self. Man is busy with things external, whether these are humans or non-humans, and he is obliged by the very structure of this Subtle Body to engross himself in this business of life, by which what is meant is his connection with things outside him, and this requirements on his part to adjust with these principles outside,—persons, things, etc. Man is in an unfortunate condition. He is not healthy, truly speaking, as seen by a deep analysis into the way in which the Subtle Body is working. He is helplessly driven outside his own self, as if a devil is sitting inside him, never allowing him to think of the point from which this energy arises. So, no one thinks of his own self. It is impossible to find time for that, or even to have the capacity to investigate in this manner. *The whole activity of life, right from morning till evening, is a pushing out of oneself the whole energy that is within, and pouring it on something else, as if the entire world is made up of everything except one's own self!* This happens due to the very nature of the Subtle Body. It is like a pumping engine which releases energy externally, and externalises the whole personality, so that, in a way, man is pushed by someone outwardly, perpetually, day-in and day-out. The whole of man's life may be said to be a helpless movement in some direction which is chalked out by the intentions of the Subtle Body.

The Subtle Body is an inexhaustible source of energy. This pump-house never gets tired of working, and it cannot get exhausted, perhaps, even when one dies. It continues, and it shall continue as long as its purposes are not fulfilled, like a creditor who will pursue the debtor wherever he goes. Even if the debtor is ruined completely, the creditor is not going to leave him, because he feels that the debtor owes something to him. A pitiless and irrepressible activity is going on in the Subtle Body, which is filled with infinite cravings, and the vehemence of its craving is the reason for the velocity of its action.

The Subtle Body Is an Organisation of Desires

The power with which the Subtle Body works is proportional to the desires of which it is constituted. And, by another form of definition, it may be said that the Subtle Body is nothing but a heap of desires. This is a view very near to that of the Western psycho-analysts, and, perhaps, there is a great truth in this finding. They hold that the whole personality of the human being is the urge of a desire, it may be a bundle of desires, or it may be said, in a way, to be a single desire.

Here psychologists differ among themselves,—whether it is one desire, or two desires, or three or more desires that man has.. Researches were made in this line by psycho-analysts like Freud, Adler and Jung. These researchers thought that the human personality is made up of three different structures. Man has various types of urges, and differences in the schools of psychology arise on account of the feeling that the urges are different from one another. But, principally, they are the ramifications of a central impulse, a form of man's whole impulsive nature, which takes different shapes, just as a man puts on different behaviours in his life according to the needs of the time. He appears differently at different hours of the day due to the requirement or the exigency of a particular occasion. But, he is not different persons; he is the same person. Man reveals a fraction of his personality when he behaves in a particular way or puts on a special mood. Likewise, it may be said that these impulses, these desires! these urges, are not necessarily different sections compartmentalised by the psyche, but they are facets, as it were, of a single diamond, each one reflecting the other, and each one contributing to form a single force. *A pin-pointed spatio-temporal pressure of a desire is what is known as individuality.*

Man is an individual because he is capable of being isolated from others. The segregation of oneself from other similar locations or points of self-assertion is maintained by the affirmation of a type of desire. One's desire is constituted in such a way that it cannot get identified with another's desire, for reasons of its own, and, therefore, man maintains his individuality. Otherwise, one would merge into another, and there would be no personalities separated from one another. The intense affirming character of the individual is due to the intensity of the desire.

Basic Desires of Man According to General Psychology

What are these desires? An analysis of the nature of desire will be of much help to know what things are contained within man, and to know what competency he has to do anything in this world, where he is placed in this context of creation. Also, if the Subtle Body, as mentioned above, is full of desires, a study of what these desires are must definitely help us to understand the Subtle Body more clearly.

There are two desires in man, as it is usually said by the schools of General Psychology,—the desire to preserve oneself, and the desire to perpetuate oneself. Again, the desire to preserve oneself has a twofold character. It asserts itself or manifests itself as an affirmation of the body, and also as an affirmation of the psyche. Not only the body but also the mind has to be preserved. So, the desires, which are supposed to be what are known as self-preservation and self-perpetuation, can be dissected further into three desires, viz., self-perpetuation, and self-preservation of a double character, physical and psychical.

Normally, man has a love of the body, and he does not wish to shed that body. By self-preservation, usually, people mean a preservation of the body, keeping it intact. But it may be extended a little deeper to understand, the twofold affirmation of ourselves in the body as well as in the psyche. So, there is an egoistic desire to preserve oneself in the psychic nature. It is not enough if one merely preserves the body, one has also to preserve one's psychic identity. That is why man is after name, fame, authority, domineering spirit over others, etc., which, sometimes, takes an extraordinary proportion of his life, overwhelming even the desire to preserve the body itself. Man may even cast off his body for the sake of a name! One can imagine the strength of the desire to preserve the identity of the psyche! People can become martyrs politically or even religiously, for the sake of an idea that is in their heads, and the idea becomes so strong that it completely drowns all the importance of the physical body. This is an extraordinary circumstance. However, it is a *desire to exist always. It is a desire to exist first, and then a desire to exist always.*

Metaphysicists tell us that these impulses have a relation to space and time. Man has a fear that he may be carried away by the flux of time which flows like a river in flood. He is always in such a state of anxiety that it is not easy to maintain his self-identity. So he struggles hard to maintain it in every way that is accessible to him. Man is perpetually gripped by the fear of losing himself in the mass of human society or in the flux of the time process. Time kills everybody and everything, it is a destroyer of all beings and a swallower of the whole creation. In Sanskrit, "time" is called *"kala"*, which has a double meaning. 'Kala' means time, usually, but it also means the destroyer. The God of Death is also called *kala*. Time is the God of Death, who will not permit the continuance of anything in a state of self-identity. Every moment man has to change. Are not the cells changing every moment? The anxiety of man to preserve himself has not been taken note of by this urge of time. It cares not a whit for his desire to maintain his solitariness. It shall swallow man one day or the other, and he knows it very well. So, he is so eager to see that it is not worked out, but it succeeds, and he is defeated! The body undergoes change every minute, the mind also is subject to a similar change; hence this vehemence of self-assertion. Man is fighting against time, when he asserts himself and wishes to perpetuate himself. This is the reason why there is such an intense desire within him to see that he continues to exist.

There is another aspect of this desire to exist, which manifests itself as a wish or a will to expand the dimension of one's physical personality. Though it be granted that man is to continue, he would not like to be perpetuated like a fly or like nobody in this world. There is a need felt of a different type altogether, which is supposed to be the effect of space upon him, together with the effect of time causing him to feel a need to assert himself for his self-perpetuation. Man has a desire to accumulate things. It is the greed for wealth and property, a greed which wishes to grab as much as possible from the outside world, to become rich materially. To put it precisely, man does not wish to live long like a pauper or an unwanted individual in the world. He does not long to perpetuate his existence like a helpless individual, emaciated physically and psychologically. He craves to be a well-maintained, robust individuality. There is a desire for wealth, which includes every kind of material accumulation. A desire for a kingdom is common among rulers. Kings have a desire to enlarge their empires. They invade another kingdom and add it to their own. The desire to grasp property, and have as large a quantity as possible, in any form that is permissible in this world, is the impulsion from within to expand the dimension of one's individuality.

Individuality is not man's true existence. The so-called individuality is a false form which existence has taken, and it wishes to rectify this error, into which it has crept, by the attempt to expand spatially, together with a desire to perpetuate itself temporally, also. Therefore, man lives a life of desire, endlessly asking for more and more of things in the world,—more friends, more relations, more buildings, more lands, more money, and more contacts with the world, so that he can become as large as the world itself, if possible. He would like to go to the moon, and the mars, and all the stellar systems outside, and become as large as the universe itself. Why remain inside the room like a small individual? *Man's desires expand themselves horizontally trying to achieve the size of the physical cosmos, and vertically struggling to defy time by a longing for eternal endurance.*

The desire has not succeeded. No person in history has ever succeeded in fulfilling this desire. Nobody could become as rich as he wanted, and nobody could grasp things like that. The world has not become the property of any individual up to this time. It has always eluded the grasp of everyone; and everyone who tried to control, rule over, and possess the world, was thrown out and destroyed finally. People went disillusioned. This is the saga of man.

The desire to perpetuate oneself, again, has not succeeded. Whatever be the depth of one's desire to plant himself firmly on this earth, this desire cannot be fulfilled. Nobody lived; everybody went away. While it is true that there is a desire of this kind, there is also a suspicion that it cannot be fulfilled. Again, there is a contradiction in the psyche. Everyone knows that these desires cannot be fulfilled for reasons which one may not be able to probe deeply into. Everyone knows very well that one cannot possess the things of this world; everyone knows that one cannot perpetuate oneself in time. Who does not know this? But everyone strives for this in spite of knowing it. In spite of the knowledge that no one can become so rich as to be the lord of all creation, in spite of the knowledge that no one can perpetuate oneself in the processes of time, everyone struggles! How does one struggle? In a very artificial manner. Childish does it look, indeed. In a foolhardy manner man tries to deceive his own self into the belief that it is possible to fulfil all these desires. If this deceit were not to enter anyone, nobody would be alive here even for three days continuously. A continuous self-deception keeps man healthy and happy in this world.

It is not for nothing that we hear it said, "Ignorance is bliss." Perhaps, it is so. Man's struggle to accumulate property in all its forms, simultaneously with the knowledge that it is not going to last, is one aspect of the way in which the psychic personality works. The other way is the falsified attempt on the part of the individual to perpetuate himself by self-reproduction. Eternity speaks in one way, and infinity speaks in another way. *The character of infinity is the reason behind one's love for expansion of the dimension of one's personality, horizontally. And the character of eternity is the reason why one wishes to perpetuate oneself by self-reproduction.* Infinity and eternity, which are the characteristics of the ultimate Reality, are pressing man forward to become rich materially, grasping as large a quantity as possible, trying to rule like a Napoleon, or an Alexander, or his grandfather, and to reproduce himself in his own species, in his own shape, in his own form;—an urge which no one can resist. Who can resist eternity? Who can oppose infinity?

Here is a picture of the Subtle Body, and how it works. How foolish the human being can be! And yet, this foolishness is caused by a great meaning behind life itself. The tremendous significance that is at the root of all life is reflected, in a humorous manner really, in all the desires which manifest themselves in man by way of self-preservation physically and psychically, and self-reproduction. These themes have been studied for years by psychologists and psycho-analysts. In the West they have come to the point of what they call the *unconscious level.* Man is, perhaps, capable of being divided into three layers, the conscious, the subconscious, and the unconscious. But he is not only these three phases; he is also something more. By now, we have some idea as to the nature of the way in which the Subtle Body works. Yoga psychology has delved deeper still into this subject. What does it say man truly is?

Chapter VI

THE NATURE OF THE SELF

Inadequate Apparatus Used to Investigate the Self Conditions the Result

The nature of the instrument used conditions the result of the investigation. The more sensitive and accurate the instrument, the more accurate is the observation, and, thus, the result. This is a well known scientific fact. The world appears to be something to the naked eye, but it seems entirely different with the use of a microscope. The scientist seems to be approaching the truth of the object of his observation with the help of instruments. But the object, somehow, recedes further from his ken. There remains a chasm between the knower and the known. There is a gulf of difference between the subject and the object, between consciousness and matter. Consciousness cannot know matter; mind cannot know any object; the scientist cannot know anything. The scientist has to fail in the end on account of the very method and apparatus that he employs to investigate the nature of things.

The Senses Are Unreliable

One is likely to think that knowing the self is a simple matter. Everyone knows one's own self. Man refers to his own self by his name, by his designation, by his characteristics, by height, weight, width, and social relations. But this is a description of certain phenomena rather than the essentiality. Man, as a part of Nature, forms a content of space and time. Thus, his usual notion of his own self, as a human being, as a man or a woman, as a relative of So-and-so, with such physical dimensions, etc., would be to know the self as he knows any other object in the world. Man, when he appears to himself as a physical body, is an object rather than a subject. Nobody looks upon himself as a subject, but sees himself as an object, as he sees a brick or a tree outside, because everyone can 'see' oneself and not just 'be' a pure subject. Everyone can see his body as he can see a building 'outside' 'in space'. So, from the point of view of mere observation through the sense organs, one's own self does not differ much from other objects of sense. The human body is as much an object of the senses as any other object. Thus, to say, "I am So-and-so" in a sociological or a merely physical sense, would not be a correct definition of one's personality. When it was said that one has to know one's own self, it was not meant that one has to know it through the sense organs. The knowledge obtained through the senses, gathered through perception, is limited to the structure of the sense organs. If the organs were to be constituted in a different way, the picture that they would present would be quite a different thing altogether.

If the knowledge gained through the light rays impinging on the eyeballs is to be believed, it would be really a precarious knowledge indeed. The eyeballs are like lenses, and whatever be the nature of the lens that is used, to that extent the observation is conditioned. Man has been made in one way. He has got human eyes, and therefore he sees everything as human. Every human being has a similar set of eyes. But, if he had X-ray eyes, he would see a different world altogether. If it can be imagined that the eyes are made like microscopes, would anyone be able to live in this world? And, yet, can anyone say that it would be a wrong perception? Perhaps, that would be a better and more reliable information. But the better perception would make one's life itself impossible as it is lived. In a way it appears that ignorance keeps one happy. It is evident that it would be futile to depend upon the sense organs to supply correct knowledge. The sense organs include not merely the eyes, but also the ears, the sense of touch, the sense of taste, etc. None of these can be relied upon totally, because they are conditioned. Nothing can be known by examining the objects through the relative activities of the senses which change according to the spatio-temporal structure within which they function.

The Mind Is Conditioned by Space-Time

Space and time are supposed to be one complex whole. They are proved to be not two different things in the end. The objects, including human bodies, being placed in the context of space-time, are conditioned by the nature of the space-time complex. If man were to be living in a different order of space-time, he would certainly not be a human being as he is now.

But, man is a greater mystery and secret than can be observed on the outer surface. The analysis that Indian philosophers have made here is astounding. The study of philosophy in India began by a study of the nature of man. However, philosophy in the West, in its empirical meanderings, was confined to the study of the human individual as a subject from the point of view of experiences available in the waking life. Everyone, in the waking condition, is aware of the presence of the world outside, through the operation of the sense organs. What does man learn when he is awake? He sees a world. But how does he see a world? He is aware of the existence of the world by means of various factors that work together in bringing about this knowledge. Space and time are the primary factors. If space and time were not to be there to distinguish objects from one another, it would not be known that things exist at all. The conditioning influence of space and time is such that nothing can be known except as being present in space and time. Even if one closes the eyes and imagines the existence of an objet, it would be a presence conceived in space and in time. Even if one tries to abolish the notion of space and time in imagination, one would be doing this act of abolishing the concept of space and time by being in space and time only. One cannot go out of this circle. It means that mind is involved in the notion of space and time. All objects are spatio-temporal, including one's own self as an observed subject. Inasmuch as the mind is conditioned in this manner, one cannot hope to have an unconditioned knowledge of anything. The instruments of perception are restricted by the operation of space and time.

The Mind Is Conditioned by Logical Limitations

Not merely that; man is limited in many other ways. One's own reason itself is a limited faculty. There are certain mathematical and set ways of thinking which go by the name of logical affirmations. Logic is an instrument that the mind has manufactured out of the mathematical compulsion inflicted upon it by the operation of space and time. Two and two have to make four, and no one can think this in any other way. But one cannot rationally explain as to why two and two should make four. It has to be taken for granted that it must be like that, and no question can be raised about it. This is to give an example of how the mind functions peremptorily. It is such a type of conditioning that any question about it cannot be raised by the mind. The mind will regard any further question in regard to mathematical laws as absurd. The three angles of a triangle have to make two right angles; they cannot make more or less. Arithmetic, algebra and geometry are fixed sciences. They are born out of certain intuitions cast in the mould of the operation of space and time in a given manner. Therefore, no one can gain insight into the nature of space-time or of the world which is conditioned by space and time. The logical approach, whether inductive or deductive, assumes certain premises which are incapable of logical demonstration. It does not carry one very far. An able and reliable guide in the world of space-time that it certainly is, it cries a halt and says, "Thus far, and no further."

The Self Overcomes all Conditioning

There is something in man which rises above the limitations of mathematics and logic. One knows one's own self in a way that cannot be explained in terms of logic.

Everyone knows that he exists. The fact, "I exist," need not be known by seeing with the eyes. Even if the eyes are closed, the ears are plugged, and the other natural senses do not operate, one can know that one exists. How does one know that he exists? This knowledge arises not by logic, nor by mathematics. It is not by a philosophical calculation that man comes to know that he is. The "I exist", or "I am", seems to be the only indubitable knowledge that can finally survive all tests and conclusions. The only infallible knowledge announces itself as the knowledge of the self, and every other knowledge is liable to further amendation, as, for example, in the advancement of the methods of science. Nature has been defined in hundreds of ways by scientific observations. What today is an infallible truth for science becomes tomorrow an outgrown, outmoded knowledge, to be supplanted by another observation altogether. Science goes on repeating its experiments and discovering newer and newer phenomena. What was truth yesterday is not necessarily so today. Science has not yet come to a conclusion as to what the ultimate truth is.

These questions relating to the nature of externally observed truths do not arise in regard to one's own self, because there is a faculty within man which cannot be identified with mental operation, or rational study, or sense activity. "I know that I am," is a revelation rather than a logical deduction. Intuitively one knows that one exists. Man's knowledge of his own self is indisputable, inviolable, and certainly true, and no one doubts one's own existence.

Doubt Cannot Be Raised Concerning the Self

The great philosopher of India, Acharya Sankara, and another reputed philosopher of the West, Rene Descartes, thought on equal terms at different times in regard to the nature of the self. The doubting of the existence of one's own self has been regarded as impossible, because scepticism, while it can be applied to the nature of things outside, cannot be applied to the conclusions arrived at by the sceptic himself.

The doubting of everything is an acceptance of the doubtless position which the sceptic maintains. The conclusions of a sceptical argument are not subject to the very same scepticism to which other things are subject. "I cannot doubt that I am doubting." This is the basic conclusion one finally lands upon. One can doubt everything but cannot doubt that one is doubting, because if one doubts the doubting, such doubting would have no sense. There is some peculiarity in man which defies the grasp of ordinary logical analysis. And this was the stand taken finally by most of the Indian philosophers. This mystery, this secret, may form the key to unlock the secrets of all Nature.

This "I am," or "I exist," is uncontradictable, undeniable, and is infallible knowledge. Everything else is liable and prone to modification, or even contradiction. But, the knowledge of "*I am*" is mystical, it needs the support of nothing else.

Is this the Reality that man is searching for? Does this stand the test of truth?

Human existence is characterised by a series of experiences, all of which may be classified into the state of waking, dream and deep sleep. The conclusion, or *knowledge of "I am"* is obtained in the waking state. Does man, the "I", exist in the other states? Can one conclusively say "I am", with reference to all these states? The question appears superfluous, and the answer is self-evident, because, if these states are states of experience, as mentioned, there must be an experiencer, the self, the "I". So, the answer is,—"*I exist*". Thus, if the "*I exist*" can be emphatically said to be true for all states of experience, how does the '*I*' exist in these states? What is the true nature of the self which affirms "I am" and which passes through these states?

The Self in Dream

There are occasions when man passes through states which are different from the waking one. Man is not always waking; he is in other conditions also, when he still exists. Dream is one instance. Man exists even in dream; he is not dead. But here the waking consciousness does not operate, the senses are not active. One does not see with the eyes; does not hear with the ears. If a sound is made near the ears when one is dreaming, he may not hear, if a particle of sugar is placed on the tongue, he may not taste it. A mechanism operates even in the state of dream. And, "I dreamt yesterday," is what everyone generally says when one wakes up from dream. Did "I" exist in dream? Yes, "I" did exist. In what condition did "I" exist? Not as the body, for the body was inactive. One was not aware of the existence of the body. One could not identify oneself with the body. Man was not the body at all, for all practical purposes, in his dream. What was he, then? Well, one may say, "I was only the mind." The mind was operating; the mind was existing; the mind was functioning; the mind was experiencing the whole phenomena of what could be regarded as a dream life.

So, man can exist even without the body. This is strange. Did he not exist in dream without association with the body? Though it is true that in the waking condition an association with the physical body is absolutely essential, in other conditions, like dream, one does exist without the body. There are then, states of consciousness when one can exist without association with the body. If man can exist without the body, his real essence cannot be the body. Dream is an example, numbness is an example, and swoon is an example, to prove this fact.

The Self in Sleep

Deeper still, there is a state called sleep. What happens in sleep? Even the mind does not operate here. This is important to note. The intellect, feelings, volitions, sense organs,—all cease to operate. But does man exist in sleep? Yes, he does exist. In what capacity? What is man then? "*I am*" is the assertion that everyone generally makes on waking. But in what way was one existing? In what state was this "I", the self? In the state of deep sleep the "I" did not exist as the body. It did not exist as the intellect which was then not functioning. There was no psychic operation of any kind in the state of sleep. When there is no body, no mind, what remains in man? Nothing remains, it is a vacuum, as it were. Man was in an inexplicable darkness, which is identified with sleep. No one knows anything in sleep.

What does everyone say about sleep when one wakes up in the morning? "I knew nothing; I had a good sleep." But when one says, "I knew nothing, I had good sleep," one is making a self-contradictory statement. If nothing was known, how could one know that one slept well? It is not true that one does not know anything, though it appears there is no object of consciousness in sleep.

One does not know anything in sleep, because there is no external object there. Whenever one speaks of knowledge, one always refers to a relationship between the subject and the object. One connects one's mind with a content which is outside it. As there was no object outside the mind in the state of sleep, one says, "I had no knowledge." But, it is not true that there was no knowledge of any kind. There was some kind of knowledge. The *Vedanta* analysis is interesting. It asks, "My dear friend, you said that you slept yesterday. How did you know that you slept yesterday? Who told you this?" Everyone makes this statement for himself. Again, one says, "I knew nothing." If he knew nothing, how could he know that he slept?

Here is a subtle point on which one has to bestow some thought. It is impossible to remember that one slept, unless one had an experience. Memory, remembrance, is a function which follows as a result of an experience that one had earlier. If one did not have an experience before, one cannot have a memory thereof later. The memory of having slept is a necessary consequence of one's having had an experience of sleep.

Now, again, let us go a little deeper into this point. Does one have a memory of having slept? Yes. Now, if memory is a result of an experience that one had, would that experience have been an unconscious experience? A stone does not remember anything. The stone does not say, "I slept yesterday." The memory of a past experience,—here, in this case, memory of sleep,—should imply the presence of some sort of a consciousness. If the consciousness was completely obliterated in sleep, one would not remember that one slept. One would be like a stone, and a stone says nothing.

There is a strange mystery within us. Man is a miracle. He is not an ordinary individual as he thinks he is. Man is not a Tom, Dick, or Harry, as he appears. Every human being is a wonder in himself, or herself, and it is the study of deep sleep that unravels the mysteries of man. In other conditions, man knows very little about himself.

Most of the philosophers of the West confine themselves to the waking experience. Thus, there were agnosticism, scepticism, empiricism, and other "isms", which cropped up as a consequence of the study merely of the waking condition, as if man is only in the waking state and nothing else is in him. The *Vedanta* tells us that in the state of deep sleep one does not die, one lives, one exists, and this fact is known by the memory that follows subsequently. Memory is not possible without a previous experience, and that experience has no sense if it is not attended with a kind of awareness. So, in the state of deep sleep there was consciousness. It was covered over with some peculiar obstacle. Like a cloud covering the sun, one's consciousness in sleep was covered by certain impressions of desires unfulfilled. When the sun is hidden by the thick clouds, no one says that the sun is non-existent. Sometimes, there is an eclipse of the sun, or there are dark clouds covering the sun in the rainy season. It would then look as if midday is like midnight. But nevertheless the sun is there.

This analysis would reveal that the essence of the self, the "I", in the state of deep sleep is not one of a total abolition of existence, but an existence pure and simple, a featureless transparency, consciousness proper. The "I" had no body, no mind, no psychic functions, no relationships, no friends, no enemies. The "I" was neither a father, nor a mother, nor a man nor a woman, nor a king, nor a beggar; nothing of the kind was the 'I' in the state of deep sleep.

What a wonderful state! Anyone can imagine what one was. Nothing conceivable was man; but he did exist. He was levelled down to the condition of that in which everything exists finally. Man was in a state of *pure existence* wholly, and nothing else. One was not even a human being, not rich, not poor, not healthy, not unhealthy, not thirsty, not hungry, nothing could apply to that state of being. But one existed, still.

The Self Is Sat-Chit-Ananda

Everyone was, in the state of deep sleep, in a condition of pure being; impersonal, featureless, indeterminate awareness associated with existence. What was everyone in the state of deep sleep? Only existence which is associated with consciousness in an integral manner. It was not existence and consciousness. It was existence which was consciousness,—*Sat-Chit*. The *Vedanta* philosophy uses the word *"Sat-Chit"*, which means Existence-Consciousness. The difficulty of language is such that no word can be used at all to designate what *Sat-Chit* means. They are not two different things or states. It is Being which is Consciousness; or Consciousness which is Being. Being is Consciousness, and Consciousness is Being. So the hyphen is used, Existence-Consciousness, because no other way is known to write it down. Everyone is only Existence-Consciousness in the state of deep sleep.

If the Self is Consciousness, naturally it cannot be divisible. It is not partite,—it is impartite. If one imagines a division of Consciousness, theoretically at least, or academically, one has to imagine a space between two parts of Consciousness, because what distinguishes one thing from another thing is space, or time. Now, can one imagine that there is space between two parts of Consciousness? If there is space, who is to be aware of this space? The Consciousness itself has to be aware of the space that is imagined, as if existing between two of its parts. Consciousness should be present even in that middle, the so-called imagined space. It is impossible, therefore, to imagine a division in Consciousness. It is indivisible; hence, it is not finite; therefore, it is infinite.

Existence which is Consciousness is of the character of Bliss. Why is it Bliss? Because, all suffering and finitude, every difficulty and penury of any kind is the result of the finitude of one's nature. When one has become the infinite, all desires are fulfilled. The desires are not abolished or destroyed in the infinite, as people may imagine. All wishes are totally *fulfilled in their reality.* We enjoy at present dream objects, a shadow of the substance, as it were. But there, one becomes the archetype or the original of things, as if one in dream rises into the waking life and beholds the reality of things *as they are.* Even this Bliss is not separate from Existence-Consciousness. *Existence, which is Consciousness, itself is Bliss.*

If the Self is Existence-Consciousness-Bliss in deep sleep, can it be otherwise in the waking and dream states? No, because it is indivisible, thus, infinite, it would be the same always. Thus, essentially, the Self is *Sat-Chit-Ananda,* Existence-Consciousness-Bliss. Here Infinity and Eternity get blended into All-Being.

But, no one wakes up from sleep as infinite being. The waking experience is always the same story of finitude and all its resultant sorrow. The glory discovered by a probe into sleep vanishes in mortal waking. Where is the solution to this elusive problem?

Chapter VII

THE THEORY OF KNOWLEDGE

Introductory

The analysis in the previous chapter would show that the "I", the Self, essentially is Existence-Consciousness-Bliss. This, apparently, brings forth the same old problem of the relationship between consciousness and matter, though in a different form. But such a problem arises because of the forgetfulness of the analysis already made, which showed that man is a representative selfhood of the Universal Being. Whatever is in the universe is in man also, and *vice versa*. Then, if the Self is Existence-Consciousness-Bliss, even so must be the universe. But, the problem may be tackled from the relational standpoint, also, which is how the human predicament envisages the values of life.

The materialist starts the analysis with the world. He takes the stance that matter exists. The *Samkhya* also asserts the same, though it calls matter by the name, *Prakriti*. The existence of matter, or *Prakriti*, was an assumption which was not questioned at all, but was taken for granted. Again, consciousness also cannot be denied. Thus, here, is the relational problem, which none could explain satisfactorily.

When the analysis starts from the self, the situation becomes slightly different. Here, no assumptions are made. It is already established that the self, which is the subject that is enquiring, being consciousness, is also existence, and, thus, undeniable. The existence of matter, the universe, is being questioned: "How do I know that matter exists?" This thorough logicality to the core, is what leads to the final solution. "How do I know that anything other than myself exists at all?" This is nothing but asking how man knows the world. Or, how is knowledge obtained? This is to knock at the doors of the Theory of Knowledge.

The knowledge of an object is said to involve three ingredients, known in *Sanskrit* as *Pramatr, Pramana* and *Prameya.* The word *Pramatr* means the perceiver, the cogniser, or the knower. *Pramana* is the process of knowing. *Prameya* is the end-result of the knowledge process; i.e., the object that is known. There is something or someone that knows; something that is known; and, also, there is a knowing process, acting as a connecting link between the knower and the known. This simple phenomenon of knowledge involving the knower, the object known, and the knowing process, has roused great systems of philosophy of which the prominent phases are known as idealism and realism. These words are coined by Western thinkers, and they are not wholly applicable to the way of thinking in India, though the idealists and the realists, in a different sense, have been pre-eminent thinkers in the philosophical circles of India, also. We shall first consider the Western schools of thought and then proceed to the Indian system.

Rationalism and Empiricism: The Two Schools of Thought

Concerning the theory of knowledge, there are two prominent schools which go by the names of rationalism and empiricism; one holding the opinion that knowledge arises from within by the very nature of the reason of the individual, the other holding the opposite view that knowledge arises by the contact of the senses with objects, i.e., objects cause the knowledge. These two camps have held their stand for centuries and it was difficult to reconcile the two views; viz., does knowledge arise from within man himself spontaneously, or is it an effect produced by an occurrence in the phenomenal world? This subject has been a headache to philosophers both in the West and in the East, which difficulty seems to have arisen due to the concept of reality which each one stuck to, and the consequence of having based all analyses and studies on this conclusive notion about the nature of the ultimate reality itself.

As seen earlier, the doctrine of mechanistic materialism, which thinks that all reality is matter, cannot even dream that knowledge can arise spontaneously from the reason of man, or the mind of the individual. Knowledge is an epiphenomenon, a secondary effect that is produced by a primary reality which is quite different from knowledge. Knowledge is not the nature of reality, because it is material in its essence. We have already observed earlier that there is some defect basically in this doctrine, because, if matter, which is regarded as ultimately real, is to be all-in-all, and there is to be nothing outside it, there would not be an object of awareness for anyone. There would be nobody to know that matter exists, if it were the only reality. There is some subtle problem creeping into the root of the doctrine of utter materialism, which cannot accept the presence of anything outside matter. On the same grounds, therefore, the empiric doctrine that knowledge arises by the contact of the senses with objects outside, which has some association with materialism, though not wholly, cannot be regarded as entirely true, though there is some amount of truth in it, which we shall consider a little further on.

The human individual is a complex structure. It cannot be studied without one's getting into deep waters. The study of human nature or human individuality is like walking blindfolded on a beaten track. It is a zigzag path and a winding process of thinking because of the involvement of the structure of the personality of man in factors which elude the grasp of his own understanding. It cannot be said that any school of thought is wholly right or wholly wrong, because each one presents a facet or a feature, which is revealed when one's understanding is focussed on that particular aspect only. Man is never accustomed to think in a total manner. Such a thing is almost impossible for people. All thoughts are partial in most cases. We always take into consideration certain features of reality, certain aspects of an event; and an entire circumstance of any occurrence or event is beyond the reach of human understanding, because man himself is not a totality; he is a partiality. He is an abstraction from the total whole. Human individuality is a fragment as well as a shadow of an archetypal wholeness.

Here, one receives a lot of light from Eastern thinking. The philosophers of the *Vedanta* and the mystics of the *Upanishads* tell us that man is not made in such a way as to be able to wholly understand what reality is, the reason being that he is an abstraction, a partial extract from the totality which is reality.

Now, this being the case, the knowledge situation, which is being discussed under the subject of the theory of knowledge, becomes somewhat complicated to understand. It is not so easy as it appears. What is it that man knows, and who is he, first of all, that is the subject of the knowledge of things? By now we have a little idea of what individuality is. Man can be said to be anything, and any definition may apply to him. Hence, a stereotyped doctrine of the theory of knowledge is difficult to maintain. To stick to one's own guns and to say that rationalism is wholly right may not be an entirely acceptable procedure. Nor can empiricism be said to be wholly right. Both the doctrines stick to one aspect or feature of truth, and ignore the other ones.

Man Has Both Characteristics:
The Rationalist and the Empiricist

The individual percipient *belongs* to the world in one way, and maintains an *isolation* from the world in another way. Man has a double characteristic in himself. He cannot isolate himself wholly from the universe. He, indeed, belongs to it. Yet, he maintains some sort of an individuality, and he cannot always feel that he is the same as the world. Man is like a bat, sometimes looking like an animal, and sometimes a bird. He does not know what he really is. This bat-character in man is the reason for the conflict arising between the rationalist and the empiricist schools. As the subject, man has the prerogative and an inborn capacity to know. As the object, he has not got that knowledge,—he has to receive that knowledge from outside. Man is a subject and an object, both at the same time. In his essential relationship with the universe, he is the subject, and to that extent he is free, also. By the way, this conflict between rationalism and empiricism has also bred another subsequent conflict between the doctrine of determinism and free will: "Are you bound or are you free?" The answer to this question is similar to the answer to the other question: Whether rationalism is true or empiricism is truse. There is some truth in both the statements. Man is free to some extent, no doubt, but he is bound also in some way. Everyone is a subject and also an object,—this is the whole point. Here isthe crux of the matter. As a subject, man is one thing; as an object, he is another thing. He looks at his own self as a thing when he considers himself as a body, as a segregated individual, and he loses the character of the subject at that time. Then it is that he feels the need for knowledge coming from outside.

And, it is not entirely true that he is outside the universe. This problem is interesting, indeed. We are inside the universe, as an inseparable part of it, and yet we do not seem to be that! We have to pay tax to two governments, because we seem to be citizens of two realms. And while we seem to be receiving support from two nationalities to which we appear to belong, we also seem to be rejected by both, because each one says: "You belong to the other." This is a very unhappy predicament. Man is unhappy; he is an essence of unhappiness, though he has the right to be eternally happy. Man is a mystery.

The rationalist character in man arises on account of the subjectivity that he is, and the empiricist character arises on account of the objectivity which, also, he is. As a part of the total universe, man is bound to participate in the nature of the universe. The being of the universe cannot be separated from an awareness of this being. Being is awareness, awareness is being; Existence is Consciousness, *Sat* is *Chit.* As a pure subject belonging to the universe, man has the capacity in him to be consciousness inseparable from being. So, the rationalists are right, here. Knowledge arises from within man, because his being is inseparable from consciousness. Here is the truth about rationalism, its fundamental thesis.

But, there is the other side of it. Man has somehow managed to wrest himself away from the connection that he has with the universe, and really stands outside it, as if the universe is looking at him as its object. Then, from that point of view, he is bereft of this prerogative of inborn knowledge, and he looks like a *thing* rather than a perceiving *subject,* and the law of gravitation acts upon him as it acts upon any physical body. The law of the physical universe tells upon him. The law of physics and astronomy applies to him wholly, when he becomes an object, when he is a body, when he is a thing, when he is outside the universe. As an individual located in a body, maintaining a segregation of himself, man is *determined* by the law of Nature, and has *no freedom,* whatsoever.

Yet, man has an inward connection with the pure subjectivity of the cosmos, and, therefore, *he is free to that extent.* One feels simultaneously that one is free and that one is bound; one is in hell and in heaven at the same time. The human being is a mortal, yet he is a god.

Before trying to learn something about what Estern thought feels about this problem, one would do better to draw one's attention to the deeper analysis conducted by an eminent thinker, Immanuel Kant, usually called the Copernican revolution in philosophy. There were thinkers like Descartes, Spinoza and Leibnitz, who were confident that knowledge rises from 'within' only. They were the rationalists *par excellence.* The idea of the individual is so constituted that it could generate knowledge which pertains to being or reality. The others, such as Locke, Berkeley and Hume, the protagonists of the empiricist school, held the doctrine that knowledge does not so arise from within, though all the three differed from one another in the manner of their presentations.

One cannot just close one's eyes and rouse knowledge of the world from within one's reason. That arises by one's coming in contact with the things of the world. The senses receive impressions from the objects outside. These impressions are conveyed to the percipient through the sense organs and they are organised in a particular way into perceptions.

Immanuel Kant: Attempt to Bring Together Empiricism and Rationalism

Immanuel Kant tried to bring about a reconciliation between these two views of reality and knowledge. The rationalists are right, and the empiricists are also right in one way. The rationalists are wrong, and the empiricists are also wrong in another way. They are taking an extreme stand, and therefore they are not giving the entire picture of what is actually happening when man knows an object. It is true that without the contact of the senses with objects one cannot know anything in the world. But, it is also true that unless there is a receptive capacity in one's own self, which is of the essential character of knowledge, one would not be able to assimilate these sensations and organise them into perception, or knowledge.

There is a little difference between the analysis made in Western circles and the Eastern ones, so far as the inner components of the psyche are concerned. Mostly, Western psychologists confine themselves to the threefold classification of the psyche into understanding, willing and feeling. Though the psychological organ can be dissected into minute formations, these three attitudes of the mind in the process of knowledge may be regarded as the essential ones so far as the study of epistemology is concerned. The German philosopher, Kant, wrote three volumes; viz., the Critique of Pure Reason, the Critique of Practical Reason, and the Critique of Judgment, which are voluminous expositions of the implications that follow from a study of these three functions, viz., understanding, willing and feeling. In the East, the focus on the mind has been of a different nature, though this threefold activity of the mind is accepted. The internal organ, which is called *Antahkarana*, is usually understood to perform four functions on account of which it is called by four different names or designations, viz., *Manas, Buddhi, Chitta* and *Ahamkara*. These are *Sanskrit* words correspondingly meaning the *mind* which thinks; the *intellect* which understands; the *subconscious*, which remembers or functions as memory of experience; and the *ego*, which arrogates all things to itself, and maintains perpetual self-consciousness

From the materialist standpoint, knowledge would be utterly impossible, because knowledge is not the nature of the object. The object is material; it is not conscious. Further, it is impossible to imagine how knowledge can be extracted from an object, and brought within the perceiver's mind so that he may know that the object is there. Even taking for granted that knowledge is located in the objects outside, how could it be transferred to the perceiver, and how could it become a part of his being? How could there be unity between the essentiality within man, the perceiving centrality, and the knowledge that has come from outside? Unless there is something akin to knowledge in one's own being, knowledge of things would be impossible. Total dissimilarities do not join together. There must be a similarity of character in order that there may be a union of things. Even if there is a union of the object with the subject in the rising of knowledge, there should be something in the object, and something in the subject, similar to what is known as knowledge.

The rationalists feel that knowledge is inborn in the human being. It is already within us; it has only to be brought out by certain means, and these means are the sensory activities or the empiric operations. Socrates held the view that all knowledge is within. The Greeks were fond of the great dictum, "Know Thyself." It is not necessary to probe into the nature of the object outside. Man has to know himself, and then he knows all things. To know one's own self is to have true knowledge. This is the essential *forte* of the rationalist doctrine.

Why does any difficulty arise? How is it that this problem of a conflict has arisen between two parties contending with each other? Can a deeper analysis be done to find out the source of this conflict itself? Why is it that one says this, and another says that as the final word? And, how is it that sometimes there is a feeling that both are right in some way, though neither seems to be wholly right?

The Process of Knowledge of Things after Sleep

The way we know that an object exists, is the subject of epistemology. The process through which one is passing in an act of knowledge, is an everyday experience of people. Only, no one appears to bestow sufficient attention on it. The process involves the functions which are cognitive, conative and affective. This will be clear when one studies the way in which one becomes aware of things after one wakes up from sleep. One has to be careful in this analysis of what one is passing through after waking. Mostly, there is no time to make such an analysis. How does one get up from deep sleep and then become conscious that there is a world outside? In sleep nothing is known, neither is there the awareness of one's own existence nor the awareness of the existence of anybody else. When one is woken up from sleep, what is the type of awareness that one entertains immediately after waking? Is it an act of perception of the world outside? No, one is not suddenly aware of things. There is a bare, indeterminate consciousness. One is *merely aware*. One is half sleepy, and yet the sleep has gone. The weight of sleep is hanging over still, but the darkness of it is no more and the light which peeps through this cloud of unknowing, sleep, has awakened the person into a kind of consciousness which cannot be adequately described in language. It is not consciousness *of* anything. Perhaps, one does not even become conscious of one's own existence in a proper, definable manner. And in the next stage there is just self-consciousness. One feels that one is. And even when one feels that one is, one is not very clear about things. There is an unclear notion about oneself. The duties, the worries and the anxieties of the world have not yet risen in a concrete form when one is aware that one exists, but yet one is not fully aware of the implications of this consciousness of one's existence.

Since everyone passes through this stage rapidly, no one is able to make an analysis of it properly. Like a picture in a moving show of portraits one sees a rapid motion of the presentation, on account of which the details cannot be counted or even be visualised quickly. Nevertheless, they are shows of moving pieces or bits of portraits. Likewise, there is a rapid movement of experience through which everyone is passing after waking from sleep. One has not woken up fully, the walls are not seen, but *something* is visible as existing outside. The indeterminate awareness of the presence of things outside becomes later a determinate perception,—this is a wall, this is a door, this is a window. This idea is a later consequence that follows from one's rising from sleep. All these things can take place in just one minute. Yet, within this one minute, one has passed through all these stages.

When this concrete knowledge of the nature of objects around is obtained, there is a modification of the mind, which *Patanjali* calls *Aklishta-Vritti*, or a psychosis which is non-pain-giving; non-pain-giving in the sense that it is merely an awareness of the presence of the characteristic of an object, and nothing else is associated with it. But when an affective note, the emotional or the feeling aspect is associated with it, the awareness of the object becomes more accentuated.—'It is mine; this is not mine'. The feelings of like and dislike, or, rather, love and hatred, get associated with the bare perception of the object. This is a further development. When one is aware of the existence of an object, it is not suddenly associated with love and hatred. But later on it becomes 'mine' or 'not mine'. For instance, one may see something standing in front of oneself. This is an indeterminate perception of the object. And when this perception, which is indeterminate, becomes more clear, one becomes aware that it is a man standing, it is not anything else. A consciousness of the fact that a human being is standing there is more concrete than the earlier bare consciousness. A mere awareness of the fact of a being standing need not necessarily get associated with love and hatred. But this *Aklishta-Vritti*, or the mere perceptive act, or the knowledge of the existence of a human being in front, can suddenly transform itself into the consciousness of a person who is liked or hated,—'Oh, this is the person! Oh, when did you come? Please come, sit down'. One shakes hands if it is a dear friend. Or, if it is an abominable individual, he is hated from the bottom of the heart. One shuts up and shrinks away from that individual. This psychosis is called *Klishta-Vritti*, according to *Patanjali*, a condition of the mind which is pain-giving, not like the earlier one which was non-pain-giving. A mere awareness of the presence of an object does not give pain. But when it is connected with specific feelings, it rouses sentiments of like and dislike. Then the attitude towards the object gets conditioned by this process of perception which is associated with the affective emphasis of like and dislike. Then it is not merely a looking at the wall. 'It is the wall or the building which belongs to me', is something that follows from the mere act of perception of the existence of a wall.

There is a mysterious mixing up or a blend of the various functions of the psyche, the internal organ, when it becomes aware of an object. This affective perception of the object, or rather, the emotional cognition of an object drives one into action, and activity proceeds as a result of perception which is of *this* nature or *that* nature. Something lying on the ground may be seen. And when it is seen clearly and the awareness that it is a snake arises, everyone knows what activities are stimulated within the system, merely because of the consciousness that it is a snake that is lying on the floor.

All activities can be regarded as a procession of reactions set up by a movement of the psyche in various ways, in accordance with the emphasis laid upon it by any particular phase of its function, cognitive, conative or affective; understanding, willing or feeling. But all these functions act so rapidly that one appears to be inseparable from the other. Everyone understands, wills and feels at the same time, as it were. 'I know that there is such a thing in front of me, and I feel something about it and I decide upon an action in regard to it at once.' This 'at once' is only a way of saying. It is not really an at-once action. It is a series of processes that has taken place within the mind. Thus, perception is not an impartial knowledge of things. It is a highly conditioned way of looking at things, and man is not seeing things as they really are. We live in a world of appearance. This is one aspect of the issue, a partial phase which describes how no one is living in a real world, but a world which is highly conditioned by the reactions one sets up in regard to the nature of things.

The Individual Is Conditioned by Space-Time, Quantity, Quality, Relation and Mode

There is another aspect which is the celebrated theme of the *Critique of Pure Reason* of Kant. The universe is a phenomenon, a tremendously conditioned process of not merely space and time, but something worse, the condition of knowing, to which the internal organ is subject. It is known very well that all objects are seen as they are in space and time. But why should it be that the awareness is forced to cognise objects only in space and time? Is it not indeed unpleasant to hear that anyone should be forced to do anything? Much worse, forced to know anything? Why should there be compulsion even to be aware of things in a prescribed manner? Why should it be that the objects are to look as if they are located in space and time only? Well, nobody can easily find an answer to this question. Man is brainwashed, as it were, so intensely and to such logical perfection that no one can think except in terms of space and time. Either a thing is in space and time or no one can have any idea about anything. The conditioning principle behind all acts of perception through the senses is the space-time complex. One puts on ready-made spectacles when seeing things, and it is, thus, not a real seeing of things as they truly are in themselves. The spectacles are space and time. And, naturally, the nature of the object of perception will depend upon the type of spectacles that are used. If the glasses are changed, the things would appear different. Man has been provided with a pair of glasses, space and time, and no one can see anything except through these media. Also, no one can remove them and throw them away. These glasses are part and parcel of what the percipient is. They are sticking to man; nay, he is made of their very stuff! Man is a spatio-temporal phenomenon. Individuality is just that much. All this is evidently a very unsatisfactory state of affairs, agonising and annoying, that man should be in a concentration camp and that he should see things only in *this* way and not in *any other* way. We seem to be held up in a prison, and no one knows how we have got into this cell of bondage.

But the harassment is not over. It is not enough if man is punished only with this much. He has to be troubled further. There is something worse that is taking place within everyone, which points out that man is wholly wrong in believing that he is in a world of reality. There is nothing finally real in this world, and even if there be something real, somewhere, no one knows it. The reason is, on the one hand, the condition to which everyone is subject on account of the operation of space and time. If these spectacles were to be cast away and then one is to look at things, well, perhaps, they may appear in a different shape. But this is not to be. The worst thing that is happening is within oneself, in the internal organ, in the mind itself. It can think only in certain ways. Just as the senses can see only through space and time and in no other way, the mind can think only in certain given ways and in no other way. Everyone is, thus, doubly conditioned through the senses and also through the mind. What are these conditions to which the mind is subject and in terms of which alone it can think always? The psychological spectacles are *quantity, quality, relation* and *modality,* says Kant. This is a bare outline in a few sentences, which Kant expounds in some eight hundred pages.

The difficulty is that no one can know anything unless it is associated with the fourfold facets mentioned. A characteristic or a definition is always clubbed with a thing. Else, what it is, cannot be known. Every object has certain defining features. These characteristics are what are called the qualities. And there are many characteristics, which cannot be counted. There is colour, there is height, there is weight and there are umpteen things which can be associated with an object. This is what is called a definition. A particular object can be defined by naming it in terms of the qualities which are associated with its quantity, which is the object. Quantity and quality go together, they cannot be separated.

And, everything is related to something else. The very act of the recognition of the presence of an object is due to the relation that it has with something else, a thing which no one is able to cogitate upon. When one says, 'Here is a white wall', does one think that he is making an innocent statement? No, the whiteness of the wall has become an object of perception because of there being non-white things around it. If there is no non-white, whiteness cannot be seen. So there is a relation of the white to the non-white, and there is an infinite series of these relations. Everything is hanging on something else, so that no one knows one thing unless the characteristics of another thing are assumed at the same time. This is another difficulty to which the mind is put in its knowledge of things so that nothing can be known isolatedly. 'A' cannot be known without knowing 'B', 'B' cannot be known without knowing 'C', and so on. So, no one knows where one is and what one is knowing. The objects which are assumed to be quantities and are defined by qualities are also known through relations which obtain among things. And every object exists in a condition, a situation, a circumstance, a state of affairs, which is called a mode. Everything is in some condition. A state of affairs in which anything is found is the mode of that particular object, the thing.

Thus, mainly, these are the four ways in which the mind can think, viz., quantity, quality, relation and mode. There is no other way of thinking. Even when one thinks of God, the Almighty, one can think only in terms of quantity, quality, relation and mode. So, Kant tells us, there is no such thing as the metaphysic of the existence of God. Such a thing is not possible, if by God is meant Reality *as such*. He goes to the extent of demolishing the very possibility of knowing the existence of such a thing as God by rational investigation, on account of this peculiarity in which one is placed, namely, the conditioning of oneself in space, time and the various other categories which restrict the operation of the mind. He has formulated a list of the categories of the understanding, together with space and time, which are the spectacles through which everyone sees or knows things in perception.

There is a third faculty, called reason, in man, regulating sensory operation, the functions of the understanding and the assumptions of the intellect. Here, in his evaluation of the functions of reason, Kant is a little wrong, though he is pious in his intentions. He holds that the doctrine that God exists is only an assumption, and it cannot be anything more than an idea. The point is that reason itself is, again, an offshoot of the categories of the understanding. Then, what can reason argue about except things which are conditioned in this manner as mentioned already? If the argument, even about God Himself, is conditioned, how could one be sure that one is arguing about a real thing? Even God which is in one's mind is a part of the phenomenon of the universe of the categories. Everyone is in a world which is nothing but phenomena, and Reality, which he calls the 'Thing-in-Itself', cannot be known. No one can see it, because it is not an object of the thought or of the senses. It, thus, would seem to occupy a position which is assumed as a nail for the purpose of hanging this coat of the awareness of an object. It is an invisible nail that is somewhere, on which one has to fix the coat of knowledge. Why is it invisible? And how would knowledge be real if what it hangs on is only ideal? Visibility is the act of the senses and the mind, and the senses and the mind are conditioned in the way described. Hence, unconditioned things cannot be thought by the mind, and God is unconditioned, it is said. Unconditioned being cannot be comprehended by the conditioned mind. And there are but conditioned minds in this world. So, thinking God is an impossibility. And, if metaphysics is a description of the nature of Reality, such as the existence of God, it does not exist. Kant, here, forgets that it would not have been possible to know that things are phenomenal, but for the fact that the reason has in its bosom a noumenal root, which, actually, is what the adumbrated 'Thingin-Itself' is.

Will and Feeling Are Not Conditioned

Kant's theoretical arguments may look like agnosticism, because they strike a conclusive note that man cannot know Reality. The error committed by Kant in this way of argument can be seen if the nature of religious consciousness is studied, which he himself seems to have accepted a little later in his career. He wrote, further, two other books, called the *Critique of Practical Reason* and the *Critique of Judgment*. In the *Critique of Pure Reason* he demolishes all philosophy as a way of knowing Reality. But there is something in man which is not merely the mind which thinks. There is what is known as will, and also feeling. One's will decides that one should do the right and the feeling affirms that there is something which is inscrutable in this universe. Whatever be the argument of the mind which is conditioned by the four categories, and whatever be the difficulty felt by the senses which are restricted to the operations of space and time, there is some other faculty in man, different from the senses, and different from the mind working under the heavy weight of the categories of the understanding, viz., will and feeling, whose existence cannot be abrogated wholly. The will is the deciding factor. No one works in this world as if moving in a world of ghosts, though the conditioned intellect tells us that we are in a world of chimeras. This analysis that man is conditioned in every way and he is in a world of phenomena leads to the conclusion that he is in a world of phantasms. But no one can be prepared to accept this position, and yet live. No one feels that he is looking at things which have no substance in them. If this had been the case, one cannot imagine what would be the state of people in the world. Men would not have existed even for three days continuously. There is another affirmation taking place within everyone together with the problem created by the categories. There is the ethical consciousness, or the urge towards righteousness, as it is generally called, which is supposed to be an act of the will. Man is somehow impelled to do the right and not the wrong.

Now, the urge towards righteousness seems to be a phenomenon occurring in man different from what is described earlier in terms of space and time or the categories of cognition. How is it that one is impelled to do the right and not the wrong? It cannot be said that this urge arises due to the operation of space and time; nor is it an outcome of the operation of the four limiting categories. It stands as something unique in itself. Something tells us that 'it has to be right', and 'it should not be wrong'. This *categorical imperative,* as Kant calls it, is an impulsion from within, which defies the arguments of the conditioned intellect and says that man has certain capacities different from the faculty which is limited in this manner and the senses which are also restricted in that way. The feeling, again, is something which plays a very important role in one's life. Perhaps, man lives due to his feelings rather than his understandings, or any other psychic function. Man decides upon a thing on account of a certain feeling in him; logic or no logic is a different matter. It does not appear that he is working in this world on account of a regular deduction that he is making everyday through logical processes. Man does not seem to be tagged on to logic always. He confirms logically what he feels basically.

Here is something interesting about man's conduct in the world. The feeling is apparently the guiding factor in man. What is feeling? One is liable to accept that it is a deeper and more profound faculty than the logical intellect or the theological reason. Logic seems to be a poor and inadequate equipment which man is wielding, in the light of a more forceful urge within him called feeling, and when feeling begins to operate, logic fails. It is the feeling, a peculiar impulsion within one that takes the concrete form of desire, and when it becomes vehement, it turns into passion. When one is under the grip of an intense desire or a passion, no logic will work. Reason has nothing to say there, and it is thrown out like an unwanted instrument. It appears that one has certain urges within which are not always amenable to philosophic argument. Two of them are mentioned, the urge towards righteousness, and the feeling about certain invisible factors operating in life which are not discoverable through logical means, beauty and teleological meaning in the world being two of its phases.

Subjective Idealism and Objective Realism

The word *idealism* has originally arisen out of the word *idea*. It may appear that the word 'idealism' is more appropriate here than 'idealism', if this meaning is to be the real interpretation of the term; for, 'idealism' may also mean the holding of an 'ideal' before oneself. What is idealism? The

originators of this system of thinking in the West mostly laid
emphasis on the idea of the knower or the percipient of the
object, and by a sort of analysis concluded that the idea of the
knower is the conditioning factor in the knowledge of any
object. Unless one's idea adjusted itself to the object that is
known, one would not be able to be aware that there is an
object. Virtually, the object is just the 'idea' that there is the
object.

The trouble actually arose when a thinker in England,
John Locke, started an empiric analysis of the process of
knowledge. Though Locke never intended to be an idealist,
—he was its strong Opposite,—he, unwittingly, dragged
people into a mire of thought which ended in a drastic form of
idealism. Locke was a realist, an empiricist, and his analysis
led to the result that objects exist prior to the idea of objects in
the process of knowledge. The objects have to exist first of all.
If they do not exist, an idea of objects cannot arise in the
mind. The thought process is subsequent to the existence of
the object. This is the essential doctrine of realism. The
objects are real, they are not in any way projected by the mind
or the idea of the percipient. The theory which holds objects to
be real in themselves, having their own status, and not getting
influenced by the thinking process of the knower, is realism.
But Locke's empiricism posited the characteristics of objects
by defining them in two ways, viz., by the association of
objects with what he called primary qualities, as well as
secondary qualities. The contention of the realist is that the
primary qualities truly belong to objects and they are
independent of the knowing process. The idea of the knower
of the object does not in any way affect the primary qualities
which are inherent in the object. The primary qualities are, for
instance, the length and breadth, or height or the weight or the
geometrical dimension of the object, which cannot be changed
by the idea of the perceiver. But there are also what are known
as secondary qualities which are the projections of the mind of
the thinking individual. The way in which objects, in which

the primary qualities inhere, react upon the knower, the entire pattern of this reaction, is the origin of a new set of qualities known as secondary qualities. The green colour of a leaf, the red colour of a rose, etc., and similar qualities that are recognised to be present in objects by one's sense organs, are all secondary qualities. But, apart from these associated attributes known as secondary qualities, the objects have their own independent characteristics. This independence of the object is the essential feature of any argument of the realist. The objects are not created by the thinking process, though the secondary qualities may vary from one percipient to another. The colour of the object, for instance, may depend on the way in which the eyes function. A jaundiced eye will not see the colour of the objects properly. And if our eyes are constituted in a different manner, we would perhaps see objects in a different way. The structure of the sense organs has something to do with the perception of the secondary qualities in the objects. Actually they do not inhere in the objects, they are foisted upon them due to the peculiar way in which the sense organs operate. The objects are, thus, variegatedly perceived in terms of the secondary qualities. But objects have an independent existence of their own, with their primary qualities. This is the *forte* of the realist doctrine.

However, this very system of realistic thinking landed one in idealism, finally. There was an acute thinker, called Berkeley, who followed Locke, and went deeper into his implications, and argued out a totally unexpected conclusion. If the secondary qualities are not actually in the objects, how do we conclude that the primary qualities are present in them? Who has seen the primary qualities? They cannot be seen. They are merely assumed theoretically. Whatever is seen, whatever is heard, whatever is sensed in any manner, is nothing but a conglomeration of secondary qualities. That the objects have primary qualities independent of the secondary qualities is merely an unfounded dogma, which is unwarranted. If the secondary qualities are the only things experienced and nothing else can be experienced by us, how do we know that there are unexperienced things like quantity, weight, dimension, etc.? Who told us that they exist at all? If they are known by us as being present there really, then we should be able to know things even beyond the secondary qualities. But the argument of the realist is that beyond the secondary qualities nothing can be seen, because we are limited to the operation of the sense organs. and beyond these activities of the senses we cannot go. So, there seems to be a contradiction in the realist argument. On the one hand, the realist says that no one can know more than the secondary qualities: and, on the other hand, he holds that there are primary qualities. How did he come to know that there are primary qualities? 'So, I conclude,' says Berkeley, 'that primary qualities do not exist'. They are only concoctions of the mind, and they exist in the same way as the secondary qualities exist. There is no such thing as a distinction to be drawn between the primary and the secondary qualities. Some qualities are there as perceived by us, and whether they are really there or not is a matter of doubt. The primary qualities also are an object of doubt. They are, perhaps, imagined by the mind. Objects may not exist in the way in which they are perceived by the senses.

Now, a doubt arises as to whether objects exist at all. Because, what are objects without their characteristics? Minus length, minus breadth, minus height, minus weight, minus quantity and quality, what is an object? What is called an object is only a heap of these characteristics, and these characteristics themselves are subject to serious doubt. No one knows whether qualities are really there. If they are not there, objects also are not there. Then what exists? Only 'my idea' exists. This is rank subjectivist attitude in idealism.

The world, perhaps, does not exist at all. The world is nothing but an arrangement of primary and secondary qualities which are imagined to be there, but which are, perhaps, not there. If primary qualities are assumed to be independent characteristics of the objects, why not also assume that the secondary qualities are also there really, independent of our perception? But it is known well that the secondary qualities vary from individual to individual, and even in the same individual under different conditions of the mind. If a person has a severe headache and his mind is reeling, he feels that the 'mountain is going round. There are many such illusions by which one is deceived, such as the mirage. Things are not there, but they appear to be there. Why should it not be thought that the primary qualities are also like the mirage, which are somehow or other imagined, but may not be there? If they are not there, the world is also not there. The implications of this suggestion are far reaching, because the doctrine shakes the very foundation of human thinking. Is man living in a real world or in an illusory phenomenon? The extreme form of idealism holds that the world does not exist.

Metaphysical Idealism

Anything carried to the extreme is likely to lose the very point it is driving at. Truth seems to be in the middle, between two extremes. The knowledge process involved in the awareness of an object would not normally be possible unless there is something which is designated as the object. If it is not there at all, knowledge itself cannot be explained. If the world does not exist, there is no such thing as knowledge of anything. There cannot be a perception or knowing of anything, if nothing exists. How does it happen that man seems to be aware of something outside him, an external form? Whether the world is there or not is a different question. The point is: how is it that one is forced to believe that there is something external to consciousness? Man is not aware only of himself, but in addition to himself, he feels the presence of something else also, outside him. Even if that something be an appearance, it has managed to present itself before the knower as an 'outside' something, rather than a part of his own being. When he looks at things outside, when he sees the world, he does not feel that he is seeing his own self in some part. If man's ideas alone exist and the world in its form as objects does not exist, how does it follow that he feels as if there is an outside world?

Idealism amended itself when it went further, and Berkeley, who posited the doctrine of the existence only of ideas, himself had to change his notion about it when he could not easily answer the question as to why things appear as external even if they are illusory. The externality of the phenomenon of the world follows from the acceptance of the fact that even appearance is an external phenomenon. It is not something that is happening inside one's eyes, inside the ears or within the mind. The philosophy of idealism is so complicated that different theorists and doctrinaires in this field have held different opinions about its true meaning. Immanuel Kant considered this matter carefully and held that the externality of the phenomenon is due to the presence of space and time. If space and time were not to be there, perhaps, things would not appear to be outside. Though it is true that something has to be there in order to make the appearance itself possible, i.e., a 'Thing-in-Itself' as he called it, one cannot know what that 'Thing-in-Itself' is, because conditioned knowledge cannot reveal unconditioned existence. Berkeley accepted that God's Mind is the Cause.

The reason of man seems to have some potentiality to know beyond its own limitations. Though man is limited, yet he has some capacity within him to break this boundary of limitations. The very inference that he draws that something has to be there as the basis of even the Phenomenon of the world, is an indication of his profounder capacities. The inferences that are drawn suggest that there are faculties within man which are superior to the ordinary empirical reason. One is drawn to the conclusion by the very force of one's own arguments that, while it is impossible to reject the theory that perhaps even the primary qualities do not exist and therefore the world of objects may not be there, yet, at the same time, a reasonability has to be expected in the arguments and one has to concede that the world cannot be contained entirely within the brain of any particular individual. It is not true that one individual is thinking the world, and the world cannot be there unless the mind of that individual works. Thus came about a modified form of idealism known as 'metaphysical idealism' which did not go to the extreme of thinking that only the idea of the individual is existent and nothing else outside it exists. It conceded the presence of something outside the individual mind as a perceiver, and thus agreed with the realist. But, that something which is the basis of the phenomenon of the world appearing as external cannot be a material object. This is a little intricacy that has been introduced into this new argument.

One cannot fully disagree with Berkeley, yet cannot fully agree with him, either. So is the position of the realist partially right. There cannot be a disagreement with Berkeley because it is possible that the primary qualities of the object are conditioned by the perceiving mind. But there is another aspect of it; the conditioning of the perceived object by the perceiving mind does not preclude the position that there is evidently something behind this phenomenon of perception. This subject has been elaborately discussed in the context of the *Brahma Sutras* by *Acharya Sankara,* when he refuted the idealistic doctrine of *Yogachara Buddhism* which held that only ideas exist and that a real world does not exist outside. The obvious outcome is that *if nothing exists outside, even the idea that nothing exists outside cannot arise.* This is a subtle point that has to be noticed here. The argument is that nothing exists outside. But, the idea that nothing exists outside cannot arise unless something outside evokes such a notion. This was the point made out by vigorous realist and empiricist schools.

The difficulty cannot be easily overcome, because there is a pull in two directions by the reality that seems to be 'there', and the 'phenomenal' character of the world. It was noticed earlier that man belongs to phenomena and also to a noumenal reality. The human being partakes of two realms of experience. He is partly in the realm of the eternal, infinite something, and partly also in a world of passing shadows. This is perhaps the reason why he is caught by two camps from two different directions, the realist and the idealist. The idealistic feature is present in him and the realistic pressure is also there at the same time, in the same way as he is a rationalist and an empiricist, for two different reasons

The metaphysical idealism referred to is an advanced form of idealism which holds that one cannot completely abrogate the belief that something outside is there. Something has to be there; else, one cannot be forced to feel that something is there at all. But that something, though it is presumably there, cannot be a material object. It cannot be material because it has to be known by a conscious principle. Matter cannot know itself. Matter is a name that is given to a particular circumstance bereft of self-consciousness. Where consciousness is present, or awareness is there, it is called a subject, and not an object. If the objective world, the world of objects, is constituted of matter bereft of consciousness, it cannot become a content of anyone's consciousness. It is well known that like attracts like, and something that is totally dissimilar in character cannot be a content of the perceiving mind which is endowed with consciousness. Here, again, is another difficulty. How does one know a material world? There has to be some undercurrent of connection between the seen and the seer. If that were not to be there, knowledge would not be possible. If the world is wholly material in nature, nobody could know that it exists.

The Knowledge Process Explained

In the knowledge process there are three ingredients involved: *Pramatr, Pramana* and *Prameya*,—the knower, the process of knowing and the object of knowledge. The knower, or the *Pramatr*, comes in contact with the *Prameya*, or the known object, through the medium, called *Pramana*, or the knowing process. What does one mean by these three items,—the knower, the knowing process and the known object? The knowing process is the illuminating link connecting the knower with the object that is known. It has to be an illuminating or illumined process, because knowledge is always illumination. It is a light which is of a peculiar nature, not like others as the sunlight. It is a movement of self-consciousness.

With difficulty can one explain what consciousness is. The word is, no doubt, repeated by everyone as if it is very clear. We have to think that it is clear, because there is no other word which can explain it, and everyone knows what consciousness is. It does not call for a commentary on its essential nature. Everyone is aware that oneself is, and one need not ask for an explanation of what that phenomenon is. If the question, 'how do you know that you exist?' is raised, everyone would retort, 'I know that I exist', and no further questioning is necessary. It is just clear. This clarity of one's awareness that one exists is an illustration of what consciousness, or awareness, is, or has to be. If anybody wants to know what consciousness is, he has only to close his eyes for a few seconds, and feel how he knows that he is. This intriguing experience of one's knowing that he is, is consciousness operating. In this consciousness of one's being there is also the root of the urge to know that other things are also there, apart from oneself.

Some idea is already gained of the process of knowing things after one wakes up from sleep. There is, first of all, a self consciousness in everyone, the *Pramatr-Chaitanya*. Consciousness of the knower is called *Pramatr-Chaitanya*. *Chaitanya* is consciousness; *Pramatr* is the knower. The knowing consciousness of the knower as existing in himself, or itself, is *Prarnatr-Chaitanya*. It moves in some particular manner, or rather, it appears as if it is moving No one can fully be sure if it really moves. But it looks as if it is moving. This cautious proviso has to be added because it will be told sometimes that consciousness cannot move, and does not move, and need not move, because of its all-pervading nature.

It is omnipresent and, so, to say that it moves would be an inaccurate statement. Yet, it looks as if it is moving, for a reason which is to account for the 'externality' of the world of objects.

There is a thing called mind within man. The mind is charged with consciousness, as a copper wire may be charged with electricity. The wire becomes live when it allows the movement of electric energy through it. Likewise, the mind becomes live, and one says 'the mind moves'. *The mind knows in the same way as a wire is electricity.* The wire is not electricity; even so, the mind is not consciousness. Yet, when one touches the wire, one receives a shock, because the force and the medium cannot be separated from each other. In the same way, we may say, the mind is consciousness. It is not consciousness in one way, and it is consciousness in another way. The process of the enlivening of the mind by the presence of consciousness within is the incentive given to the knowing process. It is as if life is induced into an inanimate object. The mind is an urge within to move outwardly. It is not a thing or a substance. It is a faculty which pushes everyone outside. There is a permanent impulse within everyone to move outside oneself, to go beyond the limitations of one's body, and man is more an object than a subject in the practical field of the world, a reason why he is so much concerned with things outside rather than his own self. Everyone's worries are about the world, and there is no other anxiety. This happens due to the strange impulse from within to move outside, to go out beyond oneself. The mind pushes itself beyond itself. And, so, when consciousness operates through the mind, it looks as if the consciousness is also drawn towards an external something. What moves actually is the mind and not consciousness. This movement of the mind attended with consciousness is called *Pramana*, or the knowing process.

The *Vedanta* psychology holds that the mind assumes the shape of its object. This form which the mind assumes is called a *Vritti*. A *Vritti* is a modification of the mind in terms of a particular object. When a form is known, or an object is contacted, the mind is supposed to envelop that object. This process of the enveloping of the object by the mind is called *Vritti-Vyapti*. *Vyapti* is pervasion. The pervasion by the mind of a particular location called the object is *Vritti-Vyapti*. However, it is not enough if the mind assumes merely the *shape* or the form of the object. One has to be *aware* that the object is there. This awareness that the object is there is due to the presence of consciousness in this moving process called the mind. The illumination of the presence of the form called the object is termed *Phala-Vyapti*. So, a twofold activity takes place when an object is known, viz., the mind *pervades* the form and the consciousness *illumines* the form. The knowledge of the object is actually the knowledge of a form. The form is made available to perception by the activity of the mind, and the awareness of it arises on account of the consciousness attending upon the mind.

The point is that the object cannot be wholly material. If it is to be material, consciousness cannot illumine it. Consciousness is qualitatively different from the object which is material, supposing that it is material. The *Vedanta* psychology holds that the object cannot be material, because consciousness knows that the object is there, and it comes in contact with the object, which is possible only if it has some similarity with the object, which, again, makes one conclude that the principle of consciousness is somehow inherent in the object, also. This is a gradual deduction that is made from the premise that knowledge of the object is possible. The conclusion, therefore, is that consciousness is potentially inherent in the object. The *Vedanta* calls it *Vishaya-Chaitanya*, and not merely *Vishaya*. *Vishaya* is an object; *Vishaya-Chaitanya* is object-consciousness. Here, *Vishaya-Chaitanya*, or *object-consciousness does not mean consciousness 'of' the object, but object which is itself a phase of consciousness.*

The studies done earlier must be remembered again. where it was concluded that consciousness is indivisible, and so it has to be infinite. If it is infinite, outside it nothing can be. The idea of infinitude implies that externality is anomalous. If consciousness is infinite, it has to be that, and it cannot be anything else. It cannot be finite, for the very knowledge of the finitude of consciousness would suggest the infinitude of it. It has to be infinite, and, therefore, external to it none can be; no object can exist outside consciousness.

Thus, what is called an object turns out to be a phase of consciousness. It is a formation of consciousness itself. The Self collides with the Self; the *Atman* comes in contact with the *Atman*. This is the reason why we love the things of the world. This is the view of Sage *Yajnavalkya* as propounded in the *Brihadaranyaka Upanishad*. There is so much love for things because one is seeing one's own Self in things. "Love thy neighbour as thyself", because thy neighbour is thy own Self. Else, why should anyone love one's neighbour? What has happened to man? The attraction that one feels for the objects of the world is caused by the presence of one's own universality hidden in the objects. Otherwise, nothing can attract anyone. How could anything that is totally outside us pull us in its direction? Could anyone have any dealing with a thing which has no relationship with oneself ? One would not even know of its existence, what to speak of attraction.

The World Is a Flood of Consciousness

The knowledge process, which is the blending of the *Pramatr* and the *Prameya* through the *Pramana*, illustrates that the world is a veritable flood of consciousness. *"Sarvam Khalvidam Brahma"*, says the *Upanishad;* the whole universe is the Absolute appearing as if it is external to itself. The objects of the world, the things that are before everyone, are facets of consciousness. God Himself is in front of man, as it were. The *Purusha Sukta* of the Veda tells us that all these things that are seen are the limbs of the One *Purusha*, the All-Being. Every atom, every ingredient, every location, or point of objectivity, is the head of the Cosmic Being. God alone is. The Absolute is the only reality. This is the conclusion that metaphysical idealism draws, which does not mean that external objects do not exist. Only, the objects are not isolated material entities. Things are not what they seem.

Modern science has tended to come to a similar conclusion. Extremes meet at the same point. The outermost probe of science has coincided with the innermost probe of the philosophers. The deepest self of man is identical with the outermost reality that is the universe. The *Atman* is *Brahman.* Thou art That,—*Tat Tvam Asi.* Here is the metaphysical or, as it is sometimes called, the ontological conclusion of the epistemological predicament, the knowledge process. The process of knowledge has led to a grand discovery that there is One Being in the universe.

From philosophy one turns to religion. Philosophical analysis, through scientific investigation and epistemological enquiry, has led man to a pulsating feeling that God alone exists. This conviction is the beginning of true religion. And the various activities of the human being, his aspirations manifest in daily life in different forms, can be analysed into his basic urge to restlessly seek communion with that which is everywhere, though, to the perceptive and cognitive operations involved in utter externality, it seems to be nowhere.

Chapter VIII

RELIGION AS THE PERFECTION OF LIFE

The Definition of Religion

Philosophical studies would lead to the most important aspect of man's quest, viz., the phenomenon which goes by the name of religion. The soul of man pulsates with a throb and a resistless feeling, which cannot be equated with any other experience in the world, when he contemplates the meaning and the requirements of religion. It has been seen that the structure of the universe is such that it evokes a reaction from man, which is integral in nature. We do not project forth a partial reaction in our relation to the universe, because we seem to wholly belong to it. *The whole reaction of the whole man to the whole universe is religion.* Here is a truth, which would stimulate one into a new kind of activity, of a character which is far superior, in its quality, to any kind of engagement with which one may be occupied in the work-a-day world. It also would follow from this observation that religion includes the whole of life, and not merely a segment of life, because, here, in this quest, the whole of man is involved, and not a part of him. Since the whole of man is involved in religion, the whole of life is involved in it. This is another important aspect which cannot be forgotten, but, unfortunately, is always lost sight of in the din of the world. Religion is generally not associated with the whole of one's life; it is kept in the pockets and pulled out only when one enters a temple, goes to a church, or sits before a holy saint. This is the religion man has mostly today. Only, it is far from the truth of religion. Religion is not a commodity that can be carried with us as a baggage. It is, to emphasise again, the whole attitude of man to the whole of the universe, or, rather, to the whole of reality in which process everything that is called life has to be included, and nothing can be outside its purview.

The Religious Consciousness: (a) Holism

The development of the consciousness of religion in man, is also an interesting and wondrous process. While the whole of man is evoked into action when the universe calls him, there are degrees of wholeness in his personality. This should explain the degrees in the experience of the religious consciousness. It is not that every religious person has an identical type of experience at all times. While it is to be accepted that religion demands nothing but a wholeness from man, it is also to be conceded that this wholeness reveals itself in levels of expression, and not at one stroke. There are examples of levels of wholeness in the growth of the human personality. When man is a baby, he is a whole individual; when he is an adolescent, he is a whole individual; when he is an adult, he is a whole individual; when he is a grownup, mature person, he is still a whole individual; when he becomes old also, he is a whole individual. There is a particular degree of wholeness revealed when he is a baby; another degree when he is an adult; and so on.

In the West, there is prevalent a philosophy known as *Holism.* Though the word is spelt in this way, what is intended is "wholism". This was a type of discovery, or, one may say, invention of the thinker, General Smutts. The point that is made out is that everything evolves as a whole and not as a part. There is no such thing as a partial evolution of anything in this universe. An atom is a whole; a plant is a whole; a tree is a whole; an animal is a whole; a human being is a whole; the solar system is a whole. Lower wholes emerge and enlarge into more inclusive wholes. An organisation is a whole which is constituted by parts known as individuals; yet, each individual is a whole in himself or herself. Every cell of the body of each individual also is a whole in itself. The individual is a whole; the family is a whole, which is formed of whole individuals. The community is a whole, the nation is a whole, and the entire mankind is also a completeness in itself. So, even when certain parts seem to be collaborating with a whole to which they belong, they are a wholeness in themselves, nevertheless. The rise of levels into higher and higher form of completeness, is an ascent of the whole from its lower degrees to higher degrees. These are some of the results that would follow from the principles of *Holism* in evolution.

The Religious Consciousness: (b) Emergent Evolution

The Emergent Evolution Theory is portrayed in a magnificent work 'Space, Time and Deity', a collection of lectures delivered by Samuel Alexander. Alexander argues on the basis of the Theory of Relativity of Einstein, primarily; but, ascends to a religious level when he posits the necessity of a Deity operating behind every level of evolution, or every stage of progress in the movement of the lower category to the higher one. The Deity, in the language of this author, is a name that is given to the force that pulls the lower level to the higher. What urges a baby to become an adult? What is that power? What is that impulse? What is that peculiar something which transforms the wholeness of a baby into the wholeness of the adult? This impulse is called the 'nisus' in evolution.

To Alexander, the universe, in its lowest astronomical form, is a complex of space and time. From pace-time, there evolved a set of qualities, which we may call dimension in the geometrical sense. The primary qualities, which evolved out of the space-time complex, constitute the physical universe. The physical universe is impersonal originally, because there was no person in the beginning. The individual's perceptions are the secondary qualities wrested out of the impersonal form of the universe constituted only of the primary qualities. When individuality is revealed out of the impersonal cosmos, the initial unit recognisable as an entity, in the form of an atom, for instance, organises itself into molecules and, further, larger organic formations which are visible to the eyes as individuals, gradually developing into the plant kingdom, rising later to the animal level, and finally completing itself in the human stage. But the human level is not the really completed stage, because the urge that pulls the lower to the higher, viz., from the inorganic level to the organic form of the plant, and from the plant level to the animal level, and from animal to man, is still working for a further upward ascent.

The 'nisus' is the urge impersonal, which is present behind every particular impulse in the universe, keeping everything restless at every moment of time, never allowing a quiet to anything, pulling everything higher and higher, urging it onward. This 'nisus' is present everywhere, right from the lowest atom to the highest stellar organisations. Man is not the completion of creation, because the 'nisus' is still operating in him, and, so, he is dissatisfied. The dissatisfaction in regard to the finitude of man, on account of which he is struggling still, like a plant reaching up for sunlight, is indication enough that there is a level higher than the human. The Deity is struggling to reveal itself in a more complete form than is available at the human level. Though it may be said that man is superior to the lower levels, he is still lower to the further possible levels above.

The Deity is not a person. It is a force; it is an urge; it is an impulse; it is a necessity; it is an aspiration. It is impossible of definition, and that impossible something is working in everyone. It is impossible to conceive it, because it is not confined to any particular individual's localised body or individuality. It is present everywhere. Inasmuch as it is working uniformly and universally in everything, at all times, no individual can conceive it wholly through the mind or the intellect. The universe is urging itself upward, pulling itself onward, towards a recognition of a perfection which alone can be called the Supreme Deity. Every next higher level is Deity to the lower. Much earlier, Plato proclaimed the degrees of the

Idea of the Good. There seems to be some point in the adoration of many gods, though there is only One God. The degrees of reality explain the mystery.

Ishta Devata: The Chosen Deity

There is, especially in India, a concept, called *Ishta-Devata,*—a Sanskrit word, which means the 'beloved chosen deity'. The chosen deity is actually the wholeness of the religious ideal which one has placed before oneself as a totality beyond which the mind cannot reach. The God of religion is the totality transcendent to which the mind, at the present level of its evolution, cannot conceive anything. This final reach is the *IshtaDevata.* The diversity of gods that are generally spoken of in religious circles is due to the degrees of the ideal which different minds, at different stages of evolution, place before themselves. Manifold worships are facets of the single crystal of the whole which is religion. While the supreme ideal of religion cannot be more than one, yet, it can be approached through various levels of this wholeness. These different levels of wholeness are the *Ishta-Devatas,* the deities, which each one considers as one's sole object. This object is not just one among many others; it is *'the object',* and one cannot think of any other ideal then. It is *'the object'* which includes every other possible concept of objects. The *Devata,* or the deity one has as the ideal, is the total of the objective concept; and, very important to remember, again. There are no objects outside this object that one has chosen as the deity; there cannot be another God outside one's God. It is so because of the fact that, here, the mind has reached the pinnacle of its possibility in the conception of Godhead, and once it has reached the apex of its possibility, it cannot go further beyond. So, the deity, as far as anyone is concerned, is the highest possibility of mind or understanding in its grasp of the totality of the religious ideal. Thus, outside it nothing can be, naturally. The mind is not accustomed to think in this manner usually, and it is rightly held that one requires the guidance of a superior who has trodden this path, who knows the pitfalls on the way, and who can point to the path on which to direct the religious aspiration.

The Role of the Preceptor

Here is an occasion to consider the relationship between the Preceptor, the *Guru*, and the disciple. The *Guru* is a 'whole' and not a person before the disciple. To the disciple, the *Guru* is not one individual among other individuals; not one person among many other persons. The Preceptor is a deity before the disciple, he is the next higher stage of deity. It is a wholeness that is possible,—the only possible wholeness above the level of the disciple. Therefore, no one can have two *Gurus*, because there cannot be two wholenesses conceivable at the same time. The question of having more than one *Guru* arises on account of a partial understanding of this subtle requisition called discipleship. When the Deity of religion, or the *Guru* of the disciple, becomes an 'external' object, fanaticism and dogma may replace the otherwise lofty ideal of the Deity being a 'total whole', not 'an object', which feature also should explain the relation between the Preceptor and the disciple.

Religion Is an Experience

Inasmuch as religion requires the whole of man, it is difficult to live a life of true religion. No one would easily be prepared to rouse into activity every part of one's personality, all at once. Man remains a partial individual. When he speaks, he speaks partially; he thinks partially; his reaction to anything in the world is not entire; holy could he be adequately religious? Religion is failing and crumbling, and we hear the complaint that it is today on the verge of destruction.

Man is not prepared to live a religious life because it requires a sacrifice on his part, which is not to the liking of the ego and the sense-cravings. Religion is a sacrifice *(yajno vai vishnuh)*. It is a dedication of self. Religion is not exhausted in an offering of some object to a conceptual God. It is not a ritual that one performs in a social sense. Though religion can take a social form sometimes, and at times even a political form, as a matter of necessity, essentially it is neither; nor is it capable of subjection to formal logic. It eludes the grasp of intellectual analysis, It is something which consists purely in experience, and hence it cannot be explained in empirical terms. Religion is the highest experience possible in man, the plumbing into the depths of one's own soul, in which act one comes in contact with the very essence of the cosmos, because this Deity that is mentioned, the 'nisus' as Alexander calls it, or the urge which is spiritual, that is, the uniform impulse present in all things in the universe, the call of the Infinite, is the deepest essence of anything. When man plumbs into the depths of his own being, he spontaneously comes in contact with the roots of all things. Religious experience is tantamount to cosmic experience in a very important way. It is not an exhilaration that one privately feels within oneself. Religion is not an emotion. Nor is it a psychic phenomenon. It is impossible to describe it in available expressions. It surpasses the limitations not only of language, but also of the rules and regulations of society and the traditions of behavioural norms.

This is a faint picture of the grandeur of religion, and also the difficulty of practising it. The glory and majesty of it is also the intricacy of its meaning. This is the voice of the great prophets of religion, which was faintly grasped by their followers, because, when the prophets speak, the Spirit illumines itself as a blaze of light. What the followers hear may be a word or a phrase, while the Spirit is not to be imitated but lived. There is often a difference between the intention of the founder, or the prophet, and the form which the teaching is made to take later through the descent of centuries. The prophets speak with a vision of God, by an experience which is commensurate with an encounter of the whole universe. The different religions the world knows today owe their origin to the geographical, ethnic and social differences among people. The sweetness of sugar is not to be equated with its colour and outer shape.

Religion Is the Whole of Life

The progression of the religious consciousness from level to level is an ascent of wholes,—this is a feature which should be borne in mind always, if one is to be truly religious. Whenever one feels like contemplating a religious objective in meditations or in prayer, one has first of all to be assured in one's own self that the whole self is there ready to encounter all reality. The religious requirement is more than performing a duty that is incumbent on a person. Religion is not a social duty that man is expected to carry out by outward mandate. Nobody has asked anyone to be religious by force. Man has to be religious in his own self, not that others have expected him to be alien to his nature. The human individual is basically religious because of the very structure of his being, the nature of his personality, and the type of relationship that obtains between him and the universe. Man cannot but be religious.

People can deny the validity of religion as if it is a profession to which one can cling, or which one can throw out at will. Religion is cried down these days by an erroneous interpretation of the secularist attitude. The travesty of affairs seems to be that religion has been deprived of its soul, and its lifeless skeleton parades as the aim of spiritual pursuits. No one, naturally, would have an attraction for a mechanised scaffolding bereft of vitality. The unfortunate dissatisfaction that a section of humanity is likely to evince in regard to religion may be attributed to the devitalised form of religion that struts in the form of the popular 'isms' of mankind, which are parochial segmentations of the social outlook of man, and which are mostly a far cry from the spirit of religion. To be able to live without religion would be to be able to live without a soul. Religion is the language of the spirit in man. It is the urge of the soul within, the response of the whole that is man to the call of the Absolute.

Religion is the whole of man responding to the whole of reality. If this is forgotten, religion fails; then, one would feel that one's feet are not touching the ground. When one enters the religious consciousness, in any degree whatever, one gets transported totally. The soul is in a state of rapture. One is then in a large sea of delight because the whole that is above is trying to pull one out from the lower levels in which one is encased. It is as if the pith of one's individuality is being drawn out of its shell. Whatever image or description we can employ in understanding this process of the rise of one's being into the levels of religion, we will find that words cannot touch the spirit. No prophet has endeavoured to describe the universal dimension of religion in its essentiality, except in terms of the requirements of a particular time historically, or of a place geographically. The universal can be comprehended only by itself.

If one is sincere in his own self; if the pursuit of philosophy and religion, spirituality or Yoga, is honest to the core, one would not afford to waste one's time with the tinsels of pursuits for mundane appearances that pass for the solids of possession. It has been seen that religion includes the whole of life and not merely a part of it. Since whatever is this world is also a part of life, all this that one sees around becomes a part of religion, so that man's life is never, at any moment, an irreligious drudgery. There can be no irreligious moment in life. In the light of the truth that religion is that magical touch which is given to the apparently diversified forms of life that one lives in the world, such a thing as an irreligious moment cannot be there. It is said that a philosopher's stone converts iron into gold. Even so is the touch that the religious consciousness imparts to the forms of man's life. What is called life is outwardly a scattered chaos of particulars, a hotch-potch of many things that one cannot easily reconcile oneself with or coordinate. But life gets transmuted into impersonal joy when it receives this touch of the religious magnetism.

Logic fails when religion begins, because the intellect has very little to do in this reaction of the totality of man to the totality of the universe, for the intellect is not the whole man. The seeker is now concerned with the whole man, and not merely a part of him, or a faculty which is purely psychological. In religion one does not restrict oneself to the intellect, or the mind, the feeling, the emotion or whatever may be the sense-oriented functions of the psychic organ. Man is not merely the organs, or even the sum-total of all organs. He is something more than what the organs can connote, even in their collectiveness. Religion, when it takes possession of man, pulls him wholly from his partial entanglements in the titbits of the world of mind and sense. He is dragged out of a mire, when the religious consciousness inundates him. One has to move carefully and slowly, when one proceeds along this path which is precipitous, sharp, subtle, and yet supremely absorbing.

It is known that the human body is made up of small cellular structures. By a study of physiology, it is known that man, as a physical body, is a composite of particulars. But the particulars are all charged into a single integrated completeness by a thing called man's awareness of himself. The "I-am" that one is, is the living touch that is imparted to these otherwise scattered particulars of the limbs of the body. Notwithstanding the fact that the body is made up of bits of physiological substance, everyone is, yet, one living, vital, significant wholeness of individuality. This possibility arises on account of there being something called the "You", or the "I", in everyone. This "You", or the "I", is the seed of religion. This is an example which would explain the way in which man has to transform the whole of his life into a religious dedication and worship. Even as an indescribable awareness of the "I" within man give him a sense of totality and integrality, the consciousness of the religious ideal, viz., the universality of being has to bring together the whole of man's life, irrespective of its particularities, into a total of religious aspiration. Such is religion, and such is the meaning of life; such is the task before everyone, and such is the sincerity and the effort that one has to put forth to achieve this only goal of the life of the universe.

Purusharthas: The Fourfold Purpose of Existence

That religion includes the whole of life, and, therefore, it is not merely one of the functions that man performs among many others as his vocation, is the crux of the whole matter,—a point which is easily overlooked by enthusiasts of religion. This vital fact was borne in mind by the ancient adepts of India, who brought about such a transformation in their outlook of life that they felt a necessity to introduce a system of living according to which *life becomes religion, and religion becomes life.* This system is embodied in the concept of what is known as the *Purusharthas,* meaning thereby the aims of human existence.

There is a fourfold concept which includes the four facets of human longing, human desire, human aspiration, and human enterprise, all which are brought together into the focus of the attention of the religious student. When it is said that religion comprises the whole of life, it becomes necessary to understand what is meant by the whole life. Life may be defined as a kind of reaction of the individual to the outer atmosphere,—an atmosphere which is at once social, personal, physical, and superphysical. All the aspects of life, which are the concerns of man, should be regarded as needs to be transformed into the religious endeavour. This is, again, something interesting and important. Whatever be man's occupation in life, that has to become the religion, that has to become a way to God, that has to get transformed into a worship of the Divine Ideal. This is so because religion is the encounter of the total individual in regard to the totality of the cosmos. Inasmuch as this is the truth, the whole of life has to be harnessed into the religious enterprise. The facets of life, while they can be manifold, may be grouped under four categories. These are the *Purusharthas,* or the principal aims of life, for which one works hard everyday, and which are the principal concerns throughout one's earthly sojourn: these are *Artha* (material need), *Kama* (emotional need), *Dharma* (ethical need), and *Moksha* (spiritual need).

Artha: The Material Requirements of Life

Man experiences a reaction in respect of the environment around which he seeks the fulfilment of his material needs these may be called one's economic needs. Anything that is essential for physical existence, without which man cannot live in this world, becomes an object of his pursuit, and his life in the world is, to that extent, inseparable from it. This inviolable·law operating in the physical universe, according to which one is urged to work hard for the material and economic amenities in life, is a facet of life, which is called *Artha*. Food, clothing, shelter are some of the ostensible forms which this pressure of life takes. Man has to work for this purpose, for the daily bread that he requires, for the clothings he has to put on, and the shelter that he needs for security. This is an important requirement indeed; the material necessities of life, the creature comforts, so-called. This urge towards the acquisition of material requirements is also to be transformed into a religious discipline, because religion is the whole of life, and here is a part of its demands. Even if one works for one's bread, in a factory, in a school or a college, it is religion that one is living, for material forces are one pedestal in the gamut of ascent to Reality. *Anna is Brahma*, says the Upanishad. Matter is one rung in the ladder of development into the spirit of the cosmos. There is nothing unspiritual in a world animated by a universal consciousness, with which every individual is inextricably related. The word 'secular', as meaning the 'unspiritual', cannot exist in the dictionary of creation.

Kama: The Emotional Needs of Man

Together with the material requirements of man, which are economic in their nature, he has other longings within, which also constitute a part of his life. He cannot be satisfied merely with bread, clothing, and a house to live in. Even if man has all these, he would still be in search of something else. This is because man is a complex of different layers of involvement. There are aesthetic desires. There is an impulse for love and appreciation of beauty. This cannot be regarded as an unimportant aspect of life. Its voice is as vehement and pressing as the call for material comfort. Man is stimulated by the impulse for beautiful things. The attraction for fine arts and literature is an outer form which this inward impulse for aesthetic enjoyment takes in him. Man has a vital desire apart from a physical need: He loves, and expects love. This impulse also has to be converted into a religious experience and performance. Man's vital satisfactions and fulfilment of emotional needs are a part of his religious life. Else, his existence becomes segmented and partial, and not a whole which religion ought to be. The aesthetic impulse is called *Kama*, usually translated as desire. *Kama*, while it can be regarded as any kind of love or longing, is essentially a vital urge which has many expressions. The romantic impulse; the aesthetic impulse; the love for order, system, beauty, regularity and perfection; all these come under the category of *Kama*. Its major thrust is, however, in the impetuosity of the sexual hunger in the individual, which manifests itself as the many forms of conditioned appreciation of beauty.

Everyone knows well how forceful desire is, and what a role it plays in one's life. The impulses have their visible expressions as well as hidden forms. The ancient seers were very clear in their understanding of the nature of human psychology. There was, in India, no ban imposed on the natural fulfilment of desires, contrary to the dictates of certain over-austere religious attitudes which emphasise to a point of excess mortification of the flesh, the starving of desires, and a hibernation of one's normal impulses. India has not gone that way, because the original incentive behind all desire is the Divine Call. This is the reason why even the ordinary daily occupations and instinctive impulsions are regarded as raw-materials for purification and intelligent harnessing along the stages in the evolution of the spirit towards Godhead. Every form of desire, and every impulse within man towards anything, has, at its root, the touch of a beckoning that comes from God Himself. Desire, whatever be its nature, and whatever the form it takes in life, can be traced, though by a zig-zag movement, to a summons from the Eternal. If God were not to call man, there would have been no desires in life. Every desire is some distorted shape which the response of man to God takes in this world. When the individual expresses a desire, he is responding to the call of God, though in an ignorant and misconceived way. This was well appreciated by the Masters, and they felt that it is not only possible, but also necessary to transform the desires into a religious and a spiritual technique. Desires are to be channelised, sublimated, and turned back to their original source, from the present reflected, contorted shape which they have taken in their ill-calculated relationship with an external world. A desire, while it is apparently directed towards the fulfilment of an objective satisfsaction, actually arises from a need for universal experience. It is not the object that is calling man when he desires something. It is, rather, the universal that is speaking to him. But, as he is placed in space and time, and the space-time complex externalises even the universal, God Himself appears as an object of sense. That is why the divine aspiration to return to God takes the form of a desire for an unrelated object. Man is innocent essentially, but he looks like a devil when he co-operates, due to lack of proper education, with this externalising impulse which pulls him in the direction of localised objects, rather than towards the original universality of existence. This truth of life is the reason why the ancient seers formulated a scheme of living, according to which physical and vital desires can and must be transformed into a spiritual discipline.

Dharma: The Ethical Law of Rectitude and Justice

But, this permission and concession given to the desires to fulfil themselves is to be conditioned by a great rule or law, called *Dharma*. If *Dharma*, the principle of the righteousness of the law, does not regulate the operation of desires, they cease to be aids in the movement of the spirit towards God. Regulated desire is not an obstacle. It is, rather, the dynamo that pumps energy into the human system and enables man to live a healthy life of constructive activity. Waters of a river, which are accumulated by the construction of a dam, can be either utilised for the beneficial purpose of agriculture, or they may burst forth into a destructive activity, damaging villages and killing people. Even so with desires, which are like flowing rivers, and which get dammed up when they are bottled inside the individuality of a man. They are intended for focussing the mind and concentration of it for driving the individual towards the universal Reality, and not to be dissipated in any grossly outward movement of the urge for unmitigated indulgence of a spatio-temporal character.

Dharma is law, righteousness, virtue, or a regulative principle, which harmonises everything with everything else. The individual cannot escape a little of selfishness because of the affirmation of the individuality which is turbulent. There is an urge within everyone to maintain one's own self to the detriment of others, a form which desire takes when it is concentrated within the body, and ignores the presence of other individuals of a similar nature. *Dharma*, or law, insists that desire can be fulfilled, but not to the disadvantage of others who also exist in this world, and who too have a similar permission to fulfil their desires. "Do unto others as you would be done by." "Do not do to others what you would not like to be done to yourself." If one wishes that everything should belong to oneself, everyone else also can entertain a similar wish. If everyone wishes to have everything for one's own self, what would be the result? There would be chaos and destruction. Law is the principle of cooperation in life as against competition, conflict, battle and war. It is the concession which each individual is expected to make in respect of every other individual in the world, because the world is a 'Kingdom of Ends,' and not a restless flow of 'means' only. Each individual has a status of his own, or her own, or its own, and no individual is a means to another individual. Exploitation is not permitted by the very structure of the world. No one can utilise another for one's own purpose, or satisfaction. Because, desire, whatever be its nature, has a peculiar trait of exploiting others. Whenever a desire arises in man, he has a subtle inkling to utilise others for the fulfilment of that impulse. And when the desire becomes intense, violent, and takes the form of an unruly passion, it may wholly ignore the welfare of others, and may even tend towards the other form of it, namely a desire to destroy. To prevent such a possible catastrophe, a regimentation has to be introduced into one's life.

In the *Bhagavadgita*, there is a reference to this principle of the permission given for the fulfilment of desire provided it is not contrary to law: *Dharmaviruddho bhuteshu kamosmi*, "I am that desire in man which is not against the operation of law, which is in conformity with the principle of righteousness." What is righteousness? What is law, and what is *Dharma*, which has to condition desire, and in harmony with which desire is permissible in life? In the *Veda*, there are two significant terms used: *Satya* and *Rita*. *Satya* is the law of the Absolute. *Rita* is the very same law operating in the cosmos as a regulative principle, immanent in all things. And every law that man can think of in his mind is a fraction of this cosmic law which is rooted in the integrality of the universal. There is a necessity to introduce a system of coherence among the visible particulars, so that they form a harmonious whole, a hierarchy of completeness and not a mess of jarring notes without any relation among themselves. The individuals in the cosmos are not really scattered particulars. They are integral parts of a whole, orderly, arranged in an hierarchical fashion, controlled by the supreme indivisibility of God's perfection. The universality of God is the reason behind the need to implement a law of harmony among the individualities in the world. Law exists because God exists, and law is the way in which God's Indivisible Being manifests itself through space and time. It is the cementing factor in life, bringing together isolated forms into an integral whole.

The mandate, or the imperative, that man has to fulfil the righteousness of the law is also a part of the requirement of all life. It is not true that life consists merely in the fulfilment of material needs and the acquirement of vital satisfaction. Yes, they are permitted, no doubt. But, it is a permission under the law operating everywhere, uniformly. *Artha, Kama, Dharma,* are the three terms signifying the three facets of the approach of man to God in terms of his relationship in the universe and in human society. The well-graduated order of life as the student *(Brahmacharin)*, householder *(Grihastha)*, recluse *(Vanaprastha)*, and the super-individual sage *(Sannyasin)*, is the scientific formulation of the way in which human impulses are to be trained for a dedication of time to eternity.

Moksha: The Spiritual Aim of the Universe

Ultimately, the supreme aim of life is not the fulfilment of any desire, but the attainment of liberation, *Moksha*. The evolutionary process of the cosmos is the movement of all phenomena towards Self-realisation, not of any given individual, but of all things uniformly. It is the Self-realisation of the universe. The universe is struggling to become aware of its own existence as a total whole. The cosmos is endeavouring to regain its integrality in an all-inclusive Self-awareness. Towards this end, every part of it is moving, like the parts of a machine when it is operating. *The goal of life is the attainment of God, the realisation of the Absolute, the unity of the individual with the cosmos. This is Moksha.* This is the final aim of all life. The other aims, viz., *Artha, Kama* and *Dharma,* are necessary contributory factors, the other building faces of this glorious consummation.

Here, one has to strike a note of caution. When it is said that *Moksha* is the goal of life, one is likely, suddenly, to be transported to a peculiar kind of thinking that the aim is beyond this world, and that it is not in this world. This is a subtle error that can creep into the intelligence of man on account of a temporal feature which is predominant in the very nature of human thinking. When one speaks of the liberation of the soul and the union of the individual in the Godhead, one may imagine that it is an 'other-worldly' affair. To remove this wrong notion, it has been reiterated that *Artha* and *Kama* form part of the means to be adopted for the realisation of the ideal. The world is transmuted, not denied in the Infinite.

Religions, many a time, picture God as an extra-cosmic creator. This concept of God as transcendent has resulted often in a bifurcation of life into the religious and the secular. Life is condemned either as a devilish attraction for matter and flesh, a work of *Satan,* or an illusion which has to be shunned with the force of will, because *Nirvana* is the goal of life, *Moksha* is the aim of existence. Man tries to withdraw from the realities of the physical forms of life and turn an introvert who cannot recognise the immanence of God in the temporal process, but can adore only His transcendence. The culture of India is superb in this sense that it has kept in mind the possibility of man committing this error in his practice of religion. God is transcendent, yes; because He is above space and time. But He is also immanent because the call of God, the presence of the Absolute, is reverberating through the medium of space and time. God is not merely outside man; He is also within. God is not only *Brahman,* The All, but also the *Atman,* the Self; *Moksha* is not a world above, a heaven beyond, and is not an after-death achievement. It is an experience *here* and *now,* spaceless and timeless. Life has to be lived in such a way that right from the lowest physical level up to the final spiritual state, it becomes a movement of consciousness through its gradual evolutionary unfoldment into perfection.

Ashramas: The Stages of Life

Together with this concept of the *Purusharthas,*—*Dharma, Artha, Kama, Moksha,*—the ancients conceived a formula to regulate the life of the individual by implementing a system, called the *Ashramas,* or stages of life: *Brahmacharya, Garhasthya, Vanaprastha,* and *Sannyasa.* Man has to pass through these stages in order that he may become a complete person, mature wholly. No stage of life can be ignored as an unnecessary or an irrelevant intrusion. Just as *Artha, Kama, Dharma, Moksha* are equally important in their own contexts, though *Moksha* is the final goal, the four stages are all equally necessary. These *Ashramas* are the ways of living by which the four aims of life can be fulfilled in a healthy manner of self-fulfilment.

Brahmacharya is the stage of studentship, of study under a *Guru.* It is the life of a scholar when he undergoes education in the knowledge of life, in its various manifestations of forms. Often, *Dharma, Artha, Kama, Moksha,* the four aims of life, have been correspondingly related to the four stages. There is some sort of a relevance in this comparison; yet, they cannot be literally detailed in this manner, because it is held that, while in the stage of *Brahmacharya* one accumulates *Dharma,* while in the life of the *Grihastha* one fulfils the needs of *Artha* and *Kama,* and in the disciplines of *Vanaprastha* and *Sannyasa* one works for *Moksha,* it is also true that the four get blended into an inseparable whole, and the four stages of life are a graduated growth into full maturity. There is no comparison possible of one with the other. Orientalists and thinkers have not infrequently thought that Indian philosophy is a doctrine of world-negation. Far from it is the truth, as could be seen with a clearer insight. The introduction of the system of *Dharma, Artha, Kama* and *Moksha* as constituting all life is the proof of it. The necessity felt to induct these stages through which everyone has to pass logically is a demonstration of the Indian genius. India's culture never held that negation is the law of life; for it fulfilment is a state that has to be reached by working through the media of other disciplinary processes which are equally important. It would be odious to compare one stage with another, imagining that one is superior or inferior to the other. The stages of evolution do not brook comparison. Each stage becomes as important as any other, when one finds oneself in it. Religion, indeed, is the whole of life. It is an inward attunement of oneself with the cosmic requirement. The inwardness, being constituted of the different layers of personality, has to be taken into consideration in all its degrees when one lives a religious life. The inwardness is of a graded form. There is no sudden contact of one level with the rest of reality. Man, as an individual, is formed of several psychic vestures, each of which has to be paid its due, which is done by living the life of the four stages and the four aims. One's entire life, thus, becomes an approach to eternal beatitude.

Chapter IX

METHODS OF PRACTICE

Philosophy and Life

A study of the principles of living is philosophy. When consciousness is able to set itself in harmony with these principles, it becomes a philosophical life. While man is accustomed to regard religion and its practice as a holy act of the spirit, or a concentrated effort of the mind, which is in no way related to the practical life of the world, the truth of the matter seems far from this popular belief. Man is not a child of God for a few days alone, or only for a few hours of the day. His participation in the nature of reality is not a work that he performs like an employee in a corporation, but it is an affirmation of what is his essential status and very being. The intrinsic significance of the person does not change with vocations or the calls of social engagement.

The Theory of Karma

How does it happen that the human individual, nevertheless, looks only a partial abstraction from reality? The answer to some extent can be had if the doctrine of *Karma* is analysed carefully. The conclusion of the systems of thought in India, except the *Charvaka* or the thoroughgoing materialist, is that human individuality is a form assumed by the effects of *Karmas* done in the past. The personality is itself a bundle of these forces. *Karma* is a concentrated point of the force of desire-impulsions grouping themselves into a body or an organism. There is a parallel to this thought in the philosophy of *Leibnitz,* who regarded every individual as a monad, i.e., a centre of force, and not a hard substance closed within itself.

Karma is a term whose meaning has been much misunderstood, and it has been associated with every event or occurrence. The dictionary meaning of it would be 'action', or 'that which is done', or 'what one does'. But, this is not a sufficient coverage of the definition. *Karma,* amounts to an interference with the harmony of Nature, somewhat like one's coming in contact with a high voltage electrical field. The moment one touches its corner, it gives one a kick, and a jolt follows. Self-contained energies do not brook interference, for the field maintains an equilibrium, a balance of its own.

The universe may be compared to an ocean of force. When individuals are considered as points of force, it would follow that the whole of creation also has to be a mass of this force, a large sea of energy. It is constituted in the nature of an organism so that it successfully struggles to maintain its identity. Physiologists and biologists say that even at a little prick that one may feel at the sole of the foot from a thorn, there is an entire disturbance of the whole organism. The forces of the body are at war with this occurrence. There is an effort of the cumulative organism to throw out the enemy that has entered the system. Any interference with the system is not tolerated. The human body is a miniature cosmos. A study of the human system can suggest ways leading to the knowledge of what the universe is made of, and conversely, if the universe is known, one also knows one's self. Man is a microcosm, while the universe is the macrocosm. This balance, which is the universe, is a perfect equilibrium of being.

What is called action, *Karma*, activity, movement, doing, is a kind of interference with this balance, which is the reason why it sets up a reaction, comparable to the reaction caused by one's own body when a thorn pricks the foot. The thorn coming in contact with the foot is the extraneous action, the activity, or, anything that one does, or anything that anyone does anywhere. The reaction of the organism to this event is the *Karma,* the nemesis of retribution. The nature of the reaction, its quantity as well as quality, will depend upon the nature and intensity of the interference; even as when an enemy attacks a country, the reaction will depend upon the extent of the invasion. Thus, *Karma* has a cosmic connotation, and it is not merely a little bit of sweeping or washing that one does in daily life. It is a metaphysical reality and not merely a movement of bodily limbs, with which *Karma,* or activity, is generally identified, perfunctorily.

The so-called individuality is known to be a myth ultimately in the light of the structure of the universe which is a self-sufficient whole. Inasmuch as the universe is a completeness, it includes within its existence everything that is substantial in the individual. If anything exists as a reality in the individual, it has to be a part of the universe. *There cannot be an individuality outside the universe.* The universe is the name given to the totality of being, and, therefore, it should include within its comprehension, everything that anything can be, including all humanity and all things.

The assertion of the individuality of a person, or even the notion of the presence of something isolated, is repugnant to the constitution of the universe. There cannot be something redundant hanging on in the human body. Such a thing is resented. We call this foreign matter. A thing that does not actually belong to the body is foreign to it; it is a toxin that has to be rejected, and cannot be tolerated for a second. Likewise, egoistic individuality stands in the position of an irreconcilable element to the universe; it is a foreign matter, and the powers do not tolerate its presence. The ego is an anathema to the cosmos. It is almost like a citizen in a country asserting total independence and defying all laws of the government, as if he does not belong to the nation at all. He becomes a toxin to the administration and he has to be expelled, because he has not become a part of the organism which is the governmental structure. He is not a citizen, and he cannot be tolerated. A moment's existence of his is a pain to the organism. So does this organism of the administration of the universe not tolerate the presence of such a thing as individuality, which is a myth before it. It is a hobgoblin, and it cannot be there. But this goblin of the individual struggles to maintain its character of an apparition, and interferes with the healthy assertion of the universe.

From this study it would appear that even a personal action is a myth; it cannot exist on its own right. If the individual, finally, is a chimera, action also goes with it. It looks that man is in a world of illusions. Do we live in a real world? Man is not permitted to affirm himself in the way he is doing everyday, for it is contrary to the law of things. His existence as an isolated individual is against the operating law. Thus it is that Nature kicks him back, and this repercussion is the law of *Karma* operating inexorably, and one has to pay for it, indeed, through one's nose.

The situation would reveal that the individual is an abstraction from the whole, in a very special sense. Some of the features of reality are taken into consideration at the time of the formation of individuality, and every other aspect is ignored, just as, when one has an attraction for an object, one sees in its presence only those forms which are conducive to one's relationship with it, and every other characteristic of it is rejected. Anything that belongs to oneself is beautiful, and what one hates is ugly, because those contours which are suitable to the particular mood, or the mode of the mind, accepted at that particular moment, are imposed upon the object, under the pressure of a psychological exigency. This reaction that the universe is vigilant to pay back to any kind of interference with its harmony, is *Karma,* which is, thus, a cosmic occurrence and not just an individual affair. From this point of view, the individual would have to be defined as an effect that has been projected by the character of a reaction from reality. The individual can exist only so long as the momentum of this reaction persists *(Prarabdha-Karma)*. When the reaction ceases, when the pressure of it is lifted, individuality evaporates, and attains liberation from the ondage of isolation.

This little bit of an abstraction of force, that is extracted from the total of the universe, for the formation of the ndividuality, is called *Prarabdha-Karma*. And one can exist is a bodily individual so long as this selective operation ontinues, and when it is over, one is also no more. What is alled physical death is the cessation of the momentum of a given form of the force, which created this physical ndividuality, and then the form ceases, its purpose being ulfilled. But, since its other forms do not always get worked out in one life, there can be rebirth into a newly conceived orm. The chain can be an endless one if *Karma* accumulates tself repeatedly due to freshly formed desires in the ubsequent incarnation. If this does not happen due to the rise of knowledge, salvation is attained in eternal life.

The Last Thought Is Said to Determine the Future

It has been said that man's future life depends on the path he follows in the course of his present life, and it is also held hat the last thought determines the trans-empirical future of he individual. No one can say exactly when this last thought would occur, as no one knows the time when the last moment will come. It is so because the future is severed by the present ttachment to the local body and its relations. There would, hen, be no point in postponing the spiritual ideal of the meditation of consciousness to a future moment, the point of lying, since the future is unknown. The undecided future would be enough caution instilled into our minds to be prepared for the last moment, as if it is every moment of the lay. For a sensible person, every moment is the last moment. t is only the foolhardy go-lucky that can entertain the notion hat the last moment is going to be a future occurrence after several years. If it is true that the last thought will decide what man shall be in the future, he should be careful enough to see what would be the nature of this last thought.

This is, however, one aspect of the matter. The other side of it is that the last thought is not one isolated link in a chain of different kinds of thoughts. The last thought is not a single thought. The object of meditation, as already seen, is not one among the many objects. It is a supreme object which includes the concepts of every other object in the world. Similarly, the last thought is not one among the many thoughts. It is the wholeness which the mind assumes by including within itself all the earlier processes through which it has passed in the sojourn of life. As when a man grows up into a mature adult he has included in this maturity of his personality all the earlier stages, and the mature adult condition is not merely one stage among the *many* earlier ones,—it is all the stages,—so is the last thought all the thoughts. The conduct of man, the way in which he has lived through his life here, will decide the nature of the last thought. As the fruit of a tree is the culminating maturity of the growth of the tree, one's last thought can be said to be the fruit that has ripened through the maturity of the tree of one's life.

The Last Moment Is like Standing Before the Supreme Judge

At the time of passing, the last moment, man gets gathered up into a total force, even without his knowing what is happening to him. When oneI is getting drowned in the waters, and there seems to be no hope of survival, when one has lost everything in this world, and life itself is at stake, when one is at the moment of leaving the world, one gets gathered up into a concentrated jet of indivisible focussing of motion. This gathering up of whatever man has been, at the time he leaves this world, would look like his preparation to present himself before the Supreme Judge of creation. One stands alone at that moment, and one stands alone in a literal sense, stripped of every association,—a condition which may be frightening even to imagine. One gets disillusioned at that moment, and one would not know what to think. Many times one becomes unconscious at the time of passing, but it is not always the case. The last thought is that idea which preponderates at the last conscious moment before entering nto a state of oblivion. The fear of the severance of all relationship at this moment strikes like a thunderbolt, which is he reason why one becomes unconscious mostly. The snapping of the links of relation is stupefying, for it was the only sustenance of the individual in its life of attachment and revelry.

One Should Be Always Prepared for the Last Moment

Anyone could imagine from this circumstance that man mostly leads an unnatural life throughout his social career. The present state of earthly consciousness may safely be regarded as a passing phenomenon, an appearance. The truth comes out when one is about to leave this world. It is sometimes easy to live in a fool's paradise, but that everyone has been living such a life will be shown when one is compelled to stand alone before the aloneness of reality. To live in this world is really a terrible thing. It is not always milk and honey, and it is not such a joy and a satisfaction as the unwise may think. Instead of forcibly getting huddled up into this corner of an unpleasant isolation where one is deprived of every help, from outside, anyone endowed with a little discrimination of this true predicament here would do well to prepare oneself for this ordeal, the time of the great trial that one has to face, one day or the other. This preparation of the individual for standing on his own legs one day, to root himself in his own private status, without being arrested by a court's order but honourably by education and knowledge, is one of the requirements for a peaceful ascent to higher realms.

Sleep, death, and coma have some resemblance among themselves. In death man is drawn into himself wholly, though not voluntarily. In sleep also this happens for another reason. In coma the same circumstance supervenes under different causes. They differ from one another in other respects, though there is a feature of similarity in them in the sense that the individual gets withdrawn into himself in these states. In a sense, deep meditation is a state of conscious death, or a conscious sleep, and a conscious dissociation of oneself from every relationship with externals. But no one would be happy to be forced into this circumstance. It would be an honour on one's part to enter into this state deliberately by a consciously operated will and aspiration. In the meditations of *Yoga,* one enters into this state of conscious aloneness which is in consonance with the nature of reality.

It has been noticed that it is doubtful if man is living a natural life today. Inasmuch as he is going to be thrown into the winds, blown off from his feet one day, with no connection with anything, one should conclude that the realities man regards as worth-the-while in his present ways of living are only semblances. The *Bhagavadgita* admonishes one to be perpetually in a state of *Yoga.* While an establishment of oneself in *Yoga* at the last moment will bestow the fruit of *Yoga,* one cannot always know when the last moment will come. Further, the last moment is not one moment among many others; it is the fruit of what man has done, felt, thought, experienced, or passed through during the course of his entire life. The last thought is the quintessence, the juice, the honey, as it were, squeezed out of what one has lived through in life. Hence, a continual establishment of oneself in *Yoga is* advised. Else, one would be taken by surprise. It is known that wars do not take place always, but everyone is ready for it any moment. One does not start manufacturing weapons when the enemy unleashes attacks. Though there be no apparent danger of that kind, one is prepared for the eventuality as if it is to pounce on oneself now. While death may take place after many years, it can occur the next moment, also. Man is not omniscient, he cannot know his future. Hence, he has to consider the present as if it is the last moment, and, like a good child, be ready by making necessary preparations, lest he should be surprised by unexpected summons.

The Spirit of Religion Must Saturate One's Daily Life

A good life is, in a way, the Godly life. Goodness is a resplendence, a reflection of a modicum of divinity. The more is man divine, the more is he also good. In fact, goodness is a characteristic to be found in God alone, and man is good only in proportion to his proximity to God. When we are advised to set apart a little time daily for the purpose of meditation, it is also essential for us to carry this mood of meditation through our day-to-day activities. While it is difficult to bring about a rapprochement between the religious and the secular, for obvious reasons, a heightened form of religious consciousness should be able to effect this harmony. The whole of life is a single presentation, and not a bifurcated community of independent units. *The unwholesome dissociation of psychological functions from one another is the reason behind the distinction man makes between the secular and the religious.* Man has emotions which are of a given nature, demarcated from other types of feelings, due to which he carries this distinction outwardly to his practical life, and sets aside a group of his activities, dissociating them from his religious aspirations. And, often he lives an entirely different life when he is not in a mood of religion. The spirit of religious worship and meditation has to saturate and seep into the secular life, if life is to become a healthy whole. Even as cloth soaked in water absorbs into its very fibre the whole of water, the apparently secular life has to become a living step to the more organised dimension of religious experience.

Meditation need not necessarily mean a withdrawal in an antisocial or unsocial manner. Nothing can be more natural than meditation. Meditation need not suggest the shutting oneself off psychologically from certain other functions of life. The psyche is a whole, a *Gestalt,* as they usually call it. It is not a partitioned house divided against it self. The psychological organ is a compact indivisibility. Every thought is a whole thought. Thus, when we enter into meditation, the entire psychic wholeness gets charged, even those aspects which are connected with the well-known secular engagements.

Background of Thought a Necessity in Practice

Though all this may appear a hard thing, especially for beginners, students may follow an alternative with advantage, viz., the maintenance of a background of thought at all times. This is something important to remember. Everyone has a background of thought apart from the way in which one projects one's thoughts when one is busy working through the chosen career in life. When we are tired, we withdraw ourselves into the background of thought. Birds retire to their nests during the close of the day; the mind should be made to retire into its background. There is a stable ground to rest, and this ground is to be perpetually there. We should not be off our ground even when working in an office. The advantage of the presence of this background in oneself can be availed of even while engaged in any work. One may have to be for eight hours in an office, for instance. It does not mean that one should forget everything else and be absorbed in a mathematical calculation or the preparation of a register for all the hours, to the exclusion of even one's health and other essentials. The background of thought should be maintained, and it cannot be lost sight of even in an hour of hard labour. An important occupation cannot be forgotten in spite of other activities which may engage one's attention on the surface. Though a person may be an officer, or a worker in a specific occupation or business, while under these circumstances when he is wholly engaged in his work or the execution of official responsibilities, he cannot afford to forget a principal responsibility of his, or an important function to be performed even in the midst of the present duties.

Here, one should be able to distinguish the essentials from the secondary aspects of life. While the secondary aspects are important enough, they lose their meaning when the essentials are forgotten. The essentials are the soul, and all the other things are the body of this soul. Even when one is working, one can close one's eyes for a few minutes. This can be done even in an office. It is not necessary to think, "I am in an office; I have to go to the temple for meditation after five hours." One can put one's pen down for a few minutes. And the heavens are not going to fall. There should be no difficulty about it. Meditation is not so much a quantity as a quality of one's inward attunement. It is the way in which one thinks that is important, and not the time that one spends in thinking. In a second, one can be qualitatively roused up into an immense strength of union with God. It will take only a moment to do this feat. It is not conceivable that the work-a-day occupations can be a real hindrance in this practice of maintaining a background thought to rejuvenate oneself. The capacity on one's part to rouse oneself into this spirit of union will depend on the intensity which one feels for the ideal, the love that one evinces for this achievement, the aspiration for the liberation of spirit from every shackle and limitation.

Necessity for Intense Feeling in the Inner Exercise

Sage Patanjali advises in some place, "The achievement is rapid where the feeling is intense *(tivrasamveganam asannah)*." Quick is the result where the aspiration is burning. *Patanjali* uses the term '*adhimatra*', which means 'intensely intense', to designate the quality of aspiration that is essential for the attainment. It is not enough if the longing is 'merely intense'; it should be 'intensely intense'. The extent of the intensity of feeling will depend upon the extent of one's understanding of the nature of the goal to be reached. The love and the feeling can become lukewarm on account of the inadequate understanding of the whole undertaking, and, often, a subtle reluctance on one's part to accept that the ideal is all-in-all. While intellectually, philosophically, through the conscious mind, one may accept this truth, the heart will not always accept this conclusion,—it will not receive this reasoning for a reason of its own, which reason cannot understand. Very few can persuade themselves to believe that this is the principal occupation of life. It does not mean that this is generally not accepted,—all long for it in some way.

But, man is not what he appears to be at the conscious level. He is far hidden deep beneath his own self. A shell of his personality is working as his waking awareness. The outer crust is operating even when one is conscious in the ordinary sense. The deeper iceberg of the psyche is buried in the Pacific of the unconscious. And unless one accepts this position honestly, mere philosophical deliberations would be no more than academic information.

It is said that after *sravana* there should be *manana* and *nididhyasana*. After listening or studying under a preceptor or a teacher, it would not be enough to turn the mind away into the ordinary occupations of life as if nothing has been learnt at all. After listening, after studying, after imbibing knowledge from a teacher, which is *sravana*, the next duty would be to reflect upon what is told and what has been heard. A personal in-depth analysis has to be done of all that is studied, or understood, and a profound reconciliation has to be arrived at with the truths that have been imparted by way of the lessons, through the teachings, or the instructions from one's superiors. It is not enough if this reflection, which is *manana*, is merely conducted. The truths have to get absorbed into oneself and become one's very being. One's very life is to be consumed in the acceptance of the truths communicated in instruction. This self-absorption is called *nididhyasana*, the sinking of these truths from the conscious level into the deeper levels of self. Generally, in studies, or during the moments of listening to lectures or teachings, only the conscious mind does function. But, in reflection, the subconscious mind also begins to act. One deeply ponders over things at the subliminal level when one is conducting *manana*. In *nididhyasana* the unconscious is roused into activity, and the whole of one's being is now meditating, not a part of oneself as is the case in listening to a lecture, or a teaching. *Sravana*, *manana*, *nididhyasana*,—hearing, reflection, and deep meditation,—are the traditional routines of meditational practice. Not much attention is paid to this requirement by most students.

Nowadays, everybody is contented to be a bookworm; one goes to libraries, browses over tomes, runs after many teachers, takes notes, and then the whole thing ends there. But they do not find time to reflect and allow the thoughts to become part of their being. The thoughts remain outside one's being. They are cloaks but not essential ingredients of one's existence. Thought has to become reality, consciousness is being,—*chit* has to melt into *sat*. This is possible only when the external operations of thought become a part of one's life and the breath that one breathes.

Mankind lives in a world which is hard to face at this juncture of the twentieth century. People have difficulty of every description. But, accepting facts as they are, and not imagining ideologies which ought to be, one has to make the best of one's circumstances. We hear it said that one has to take bath in the ocean even when the waves dash upon the shore, and cannot wait till the waves subside, for they will never subside. So, one cannot afford to wait for favourable circumstances in the world,—they will never come. The world has been of this kind since ages, and it is not likely to be something else suddenly. The difficulties of life are partly our own making. Man attracts what he deserves, injustice is not meted out to him by the law of Nature. There is some mystery in things, which we are not able to understand. Our complaints are part of our ignorance. We may have to endure some hardship with fortitude. "What you can change, you change; and what you cannot, you bear." This is a little truth, a little commonsense, which man can apply to himself. We mix up the can's and the cannot's, and, then, rack our brains unnecessarily. Let a clear distinction be drawn between what we can do and what we cannot. If we can do this, we would be learning how to live. Man places himself in a state of anxiety. Clarity of understanding is known as *viveka*, discrimination between the real and the unreal. It can also be a distinction between the possible and the impossible.

With this perspicuity of thought, we should try to live the way we are expected to live, in the light of the laws that operate everywhere, and try our best, from the bottom of our hearts, to seek final succour at the hands of the Almighty, whose benignant look is ever upon all.

Chapter X

THE ART OF MEDITATION

What Is Meditation?

The true meaning of religion, its inseparability from man's entire life and activities, the necessity to maintain a continued form of the religious consciousness have all been discussed to the point of some clarity. But, how to go about achieving such a state of religious consciousness is what now remains to be considered. There are methods known as meditation. What is meditation, and how is one to proceed with it?

The philosophical foundations and the religious consequences of the analysis lead to the need for a meditation on consciousness as the quintessence of the whole adventure. All study, all endeavour, and every enterprise, in every walk of life, results in the fixing of oneself in a type of reality. This is precisely the function of meditation. To recognise one's true relationship with the ultimate reality is to place oneself in the context of the highest form of meditation. Meditation is, in fact, not a psychological act or a physical movement, or even a social adjustment, but a trans-empirical attitude, of the whole of what one is, a perfection of outlook one adopts in the light of the nature of the facts of life.

From the beginning of this study, an attempt has been made to understand what reality is, how it manifests itself by degrees of expression in the universe, and in the individuals who form themselves into groups, societies, or organisations for the purpose of self-fulfilment. There is a gradual descent of the character of reality in the process of creation. And the aim of meditation is just the opposite of this descending series. Meditation leads to the gradual ascent of self by degrees of expansiveness.

The universe may be regarded as the body of God, the appearance of the Absolute, the very embodiment of the Cosmic animating Consciousness. The form appears as a material cosmos since it is represented as a sensory object. The world is envisaged as an object of the senses, located in space and time. It is the intervention of space and time that is responsible for the notion that the world is material and external. Materiality is the form which anything takes when it becomes an object of sensation by mind. But it puts on a new colour and presents itself in a new light when it is recognised no more as an object of the senses, or even a content of the mind, but as something inseparable from the very fact of experience.

To everyone, experience is sensory, empirical. psychological, externalised, spatio-temporal. But true experience is integral. It is incapable of partition into the division of the subject and the object. It was noticed earlier that even the so-called division between the subjective factor and the objective one has, implicitly hidden within it, the feature of a transcendent presence, without whose operation the division between the subject and object cannot be accounted for. One cannot even know that there is such a thing as the subject distinguished from the object, unless there is something transcending the subject and the object, which is implied in experience, though not visible as an object of the senses. The moment it becomes an object, it gets distinguished from the subject, requiring once again another connecting link which is transcendent to this division. The meditative effort is directed to the inward recognition of the presence of this transcendence involved between the apparent distinctions made between the subject and the object. Man lifts himself up into a new atmosphere wherein is comprehended the subjective location of the observer or the meditating individual and the context of what is called the object which is the universe.

To meditate is not to think of an object outside, though many a time it is thought that it is such an effort. It is not just shifting the mind from one object to another, when it is meditation in the spiritual sense. It is not another kind of work in which one is engaging oneself. It is not thinking of some other object than the one to which one is usually accustomed in daily life. Human consciousness which is at present limited to an individual existence is perforce aware of something outside, and this is what is commonly called life in this world. But spiritual meditation is a novel type of effort on the part of one's being, novel in the sense that it is not comparable with any activity to which man is used in ordinary life. Hence, meditation is a little difficult performance, and not an easy matter. It requires a power of will and a capacity to adapt oneself to an environment which is not purely objective, but superior to the objective predicament of day-to-day experience. One has to be able to place oneself in an atmosphere which rises above the distinction between oneself and the objects of experience. This requires some effort, but not an ordinary effort in the social or physical sense; it is a new type of effort of the wholeness of one's being in its envisagement of a presence which includes within itself what one is as one regards one's own self to be at present, and also what the object is, to which one is related.

The object on which one is expected to meditate is not outside,—that is all the difference. The object of meditation is superior to the subject, but not external to him, and, therefore, it is not on par with him in reality. The external objects of the senses are on a par with man, as far as their reality is concerned. But the object of meditation is not on par with the meditator, for it is transcendent. So, when a person is in the state of meditation, he is not in himself. He has lifted himself above himself. It is difficult for the mind to understand what this feat can mean. The grace of one's Preceptor, the wondrous touch of the Almighty is necessary, and the consequences of good deeds that were performed in one's previous lives have to fructify in order that one may succeed in this arduous task. The difficulty lies in placing oneself in this peculiar mathematical position of transcendence, and not merely in the position of an observer. One does not observe an object in meditation, nor does one look upon it as one does certain other things in the world. The personality does not move outwardly to the object. It is raised vertically, as it were, rather than horizontally as in sense-perception. As the meditator is no more in himself in meditation, he is also no more in the objects of the senses. He is empirically connected with the external objects even as the objects of the senses are empirically connected with him from the point of view of his psycho-physical relations. But, here he is not establishing a new kind of relationship between himself and the objects, but is rising above the limitations to which both the objects and he himself are victims. One is midway between oneself and the object, connecting the two, and yet beyond both in a living wholeness. The meditator has become a different thing altogether, and no more is he what he has been till then. He would not be a person when he is meditating, he becomes, rather, a super-person. A super-subjective presence would be the characterisation of that state which one assumes in meditation.

Again, one has to exercise the mind to understand the meaning of this requirement. It may appear a little difficult, but by continuous practice one will find that it is the only justifiable way of thinking that can be entertained, and all the other ways will look drab and meaningless in comparison. Even as it would be meaningless to contemplate the objects of the dream world when one has risen into the wider consciousness of waking, one would consider all the business of the world as a hangover burden when living the larger life in the insight of meditation, when the consciousness occupies an intermediary position between the subjective individuality and the objects of the senses. This is the crux of meditation, and this is its foundational meaning.

The Object of Meditation

Many teachers tell us to contemplate, to meditate upon, an *Ishta-Devata*, or a Deity of our choice. This Deity, which the adepts speak of, is that Divine Presence ranging between the subject and the object, God descended in one degree of expression. The many gods of the religions are the many degrees of this transcendent position which the Absolute occupies in the different degrees of relationship between the subjects and the objects in the history of evolution. They are many degrees of the descent, or one may say, the ascent, of the very same Being, which explains the relationship between subjects and objects in any plane of existence, in any realm of being, anywhere, at any time. So, the *Ishta-Devata*, the God of one's meditation, the Deity that one worships and contemplates upon, is the immediately superior presence.

This is somewhat akin to the synthesis which the German philosopher, Hegel, attempted in his 'dialectical process' of philosophy: A position has an opposition, a thesis has an antithesis, which are brought together in a blend called the synthesis. The synthesis becomes a thesis, again, of which the antithesis becomes the opposing element. The two have to be brought together in a second synthesis. The second synthesis becomes a thesis to a third antithesis, and so on, till the largest generality of perfection is reached. The synthesis is the Deity. The thesis is the subject. The antithesis is the object. And the bringing together of these positions and oppositions is the recognition of the *Deity*, which is transcendent to both the terms. As there are degrees of synthesis, until the Absolute Synthesis is realised, there are several gods in religion. These many gods are the many types of synthesis, bringing together the different degrees of subjects and objects in the evolutionary process of the cosmos. In meditation one places oneself in this position of the *Divine Synthesis* that is between oneself and the object, and fixes one's attention on this Deity.

When it is said that we have to fix 'our' attention, one has to be a little clear as to what this 'our' means. The reference is not to the attention of this so-called Mister or Missis, the boy or the girl, the son or the daughter, this person or that person. One has, as already mentioned, to become a super-person when seated for meditation. The seeker is no more the person that he has been; he is above involvements. It is the total consciousness that is affirming itself in meditation, the *Deity* becoming conscious of its presence, God becoming aware of Himself as the all.

Meditation Energises Personality

Here is also the explanation as to why there is a feeling of so much strength and energy being infused into one's being during the process of meditation. One does not rise from meditation as the same person that went into it. One becomes a different thing altogether, with a new joy imbued and a new strength felt within. The reason behind it is that consciousness has outstripped the limitations of physical individuality and the limitations that the sense-objects cause are also broken through. Inasmuch as the limitations are outgrown, a larger freedom is attained. Freedom is the overcoming of all limitation, the restrictions imposed on one by extraneous factors. Man lacks freedom because of the presence of things outside. Now, this object before oneself, which is the limitation of one's personal self, is withdrawn into a larger individuality, which is the contemplating being. An integration of consciousness takes place, as the two attributes of the Substance of Spinoza, or, to come to a homely example, as the two hands of a person are brought together into a single, united collaboration. This centrality of the meditating consciousness brings into a unity of operation the empirical subject and its corresponding object.

The individual is like one of the hands of a wider body, the other hand being the object. One may consider the right hand as oneself and the left hand is the object. The right hand is looking at the left hand and imagining that it is an object.

Man should cease to imagine that he is only the right hand, but that he is the whole body to which both the hands belong. This is an illustration to bring out the significance of the process in which one has to meditate on the Synthesis, rather than the thesis or the antithesis, the subject or the object. The body to which the two hands belong is not a subject, nor is it an object. The body is not the right hand, nor is it the left hand, for both belong to it. The meditator occupies the position of this integrating centre to which the right and the left belong and which is above both the right and the left. This is what is meant by placing oneself in meditation. The energy of the right and the energy of the left get both united in this central energy of the body. The right hand has a strength of its own, but it does not have the strength of the left hand. But the body has the strength of both, because they both belong to it.

One may achieve empirical strength. But this strength is limited due to the presence of an object, which also asserts its independence in its own way. This assertion of independence ceases on the part of the subject as well as of the object when meditation supervenes. Hence the manifestation of a new strength. The power of the subjective side as well as the objective comes together, and a larger freedom is enjoyed than that when one was an empirical subject. There will be a greater freedom, a greater strength, and hence a greater satisfaction. Joy, satisfaction, happiness, bliss, is the experience of a freedom that is attained by transcending the lower limitations of the realms to which subjects and objects belong in the world.

Meditation Is Religion's Aim

When one is in a mood of meditation, one is practising true religion, but by so doing one does not belong to any particular religious cult. We live religion when we are in a state of meditation, because religion is the relation between man and God, between the soul and the Absolute. The affirmation of it in life is religion's aim. Religion is not the act of belonging to a creed, a temple, or a church. It is an inward acceptance of one's conscious relation with the Almighty, who presents Himself as the degrees of Deity in the different religions. When we are in a holy mood, we are really in the temple of God. When we are in a state of meditation, we are in the church of Christ. The temple or the church is this very transcendence which is the spirit of religion that occupies a position superior to the empirical subjects and objects of the world. The church does not belong to the world. It is a divine occupation, lifted above the mundane. The temples are trans-earthly atmospheres which have in their precincts whatever is of value. Anyone seated there does not belong to sides or parties, but to the Divine Whole. This world is nothing but a spatio-temporal complex of subjects and objects. And our endeavour is to overcome this limitation. One becomes truly religious only in meditation. In other activities one sinks back into the bodily individuality. The births and the deaths of the individual are the consequences that follow from the tying up of consciousness to one point only in space and time and getting thereby subjected to the force of evolution which urges everything onward and forward towards a higher integration.

Asana: Physical and Mental Posture

When seated for the purpose of meditation it is usually required that you must be in one posture,— *Sthirasukham-asanam. Asana*, or the posture for meditation, is that fixed pose of the body which is comfortable and not pain-giving. It should not be a torture or a contorted fixing of oneself in a painful way. The purpose of the *Asana*, or the pose in meditation, is to relax oneself.

In one of the aphorisms, *Patanjali* tells that it is convenient for the mind to feel the presence of the Infinite in its own way when one is seated in the bodily posture of any *Asana*, such as *Padmasana, Siddhasana*, or *Sukhasana*. There should not be a consciousness of being seated in a posture. If it becomes an object of awareness, it would mean that it is not a natural position. When one is perfectly natural and normal, there is no awareness of oneself. When there is awareness of oneself, there is something also of the not-oneself.

Meditation is the highest form of relaxation, where one is free from tense moods, where one is not even aware that one is concentrating or doing something at all. One is completely released of all vexations of sense. Tension of any kind is traceable to one's occupying an unnatural position in the world. When one is unnatural in some way, one has also tense moods, and there is a peculiar sensation of anguish. Rarely is one released of all tensions in life. Man lives like a soldier in the battlefield ready for an onslaught, and is never free with himself. There is a feeling that one is at war always, and has to come to grips with some situation or the other in life, which is there confronting and facing one with an opposing attitude. In meditation this contending posture is overcome. We become friends of all beings. The Transcendent Presence is the friend of both the subject and the object at once, and, therefore, we, too, are friends of everyone. We become benefactors, well-wishers, philosophers and guides of all, when we are in this non-subjective position, which is the position of meditation. For this purpose is the physical *Asana* prescribed tending towards the very same aim. The physical posture .is contributory to the mental posture that is to be adopted in meditation. The posture of the mind is more important than the session of the body. If the mind is distorted, even when the body is equally posed, that would not be the required mood of the personality. The mind and the body being related to each other, there is a need to adjust both simultaneously.

One is a little sick or anxious or emotional or disturbed or over-enthusiastic. In a normal position of utter spontaneity, there is no awareness of one's existence at all, as children who do not know that they are, and are buoyant, and run about without being aware that they are busy. That would be a symbol of spontaneous naturalness. But when an old man runs, he lumbers with a heavy body. Children have no consciousness of themselves. Such is the kind of psychological mood that one has to spontaneously adopt by freeing oneself from occupations of a distracting nature. Earthly occupations, all circumstances of bounden duty, as are usually called in the social sense, put a limitation on man and keep his mind sunk in a state of anxiety. There should be no anxiety when one sits for meditation. If there is worry, it is better to go to the depths of the problem, discover the cause thereof, and remove it. It is better to be healthy first, than be unhealthily religious.

The Disciplines of Self-Control

The student on the path has to disentangle himself in a wise way from the tangles of social involvement and psycho-physical tension by the practice of what *Patanjali* calls *Yamas*. They are supreme norms prescribed by the sage for relieving oneself of obligations and debts, fears and anxieties in life. Each one is to be a judge of oneself here, and, perhaps, at a certain stage, one would realise that oneself is one's own best guide, because there are subtle adjustments that are required to be made in life, which call for different types of adaptation of oneself from moment to moment, which cannot always be foreseen. Here, one cannot go on consulting books or even run to teachers. One has to use a little bit of discretion and commonsense in the light of the purpose for which one is practising this attitude of adjustment. The most important thing to remember is the purpose set before oneself, the ideal or the goal ahead, which conditions one's general attitude to life. Whether this is right or that is right, this is good or that is good, how would one find out? By reading a book? Such crucial questions cannot be answered by the printed line, nor can one resort to teachers and masters everyday. The nature of the goal that one has chosen for oneself will, to some extent, indicate what is right and what is wrong in any particular context in which one may be placed in life. This has been broadly outlined in the principles of Yamas, or rules of self-restraint.

Everyday one may have to check up one's personality by maintaining a spiritual diary. Like an auditor striking a balance sheet to find out the assets and liabilities of an occupation, one closes one's day with a balance sheet of what has happened to oneself from the morning till the evening, to find out if there is any liability on the part of oneself. The liability is the due that one owes to something in the world. This should not be there at the close of day. One should not owe something to somebody when retiring at night. If something is due, it must be paid then and there. It must also be seen that there is no further due. Any kind of debt that one owes to anyone or anything in the world, in any manner whatsoever, physically, socially or psychologically, will distract one's attention. To that extent, in that percentage, the mind will go in that direction, and to that extent and in that proportion the meditative consciousness will be debilitated. It will not have the strength that is required for the purpose. There must be no subtle sorrow inside. All dues to the society have to be discharged, if there be any. To the extent man is independent of human society, to that extent also he is free from dues to society. Each one has to find out to what extent one is indebted to society and to what extent one is free from debts to society.

In the same way as one has to think carefully about one's relationship to human society, lest one should be in some bondage of debt or due, one has also to assess the requirements of one's body and mind. We owe some debt to the body, and also to the mind and emotions. The limitations with which man is born and through which he lives are creditors demanding their dues. The hunger of the stomach, the cold and the heat, the emotions that heave up within, are all conditions which require some attention. An emotional frustration, or defeatist attitude, would have to be taken care of in a proper manner, as a medical man would examine a patient. Let there not be too much enthusiasm about God, religion and spirituality when there is still a downward pull by the gravitation of these little calls, which will not leave one in peace even till eternity, if one does not clear their accounts. As Christ said somewhere, before man tries to make friendship with God, he has to see that he has no enemies in the world. Make peace with your neighbour first, before you try to make peace with God. These are small things, but very important checkposts on the journey. Both socially and personally, one has to be free. A bonded slave of human society, or a slave of one's own emotions and affections may be debarred entry from above. If there are strong instincts and cravings, they have to be attended to in a proper manner. If one cannot understand what to do, the *Guru* must be approached: 'I have a problem, emotional, instinctive, social, whatever it is. I am not able to solve this situation. I am here before you, seeking a solution.' One's superior will be able to show a path out of this impasse. Everyone has some understanding in calmer moments, and discriminative powers well exercised would provide necessary guidance. Under any circumstance, freedom from entanglements which are empirical in nature,—social, physical, psychological, emotional,—is necessary before one attempts to enter into this noble, sublime state of meditation, which is the holiest of endeavours in which one can engage oneself, and which is the final act that one performs as the culmination of human evolution.

The meditation in spiritual life are of different types according to the way in which the individual reacts to the concept of reality. These reactions of the soul to the truths of the universe are the Yogas. The different names with which the practice is associated are the different ways in which the soul feels its relationship with the cosmic environment and affirms it in its practical life. The manner in which the spirit contemplates God is conditioned by the predominant faculty which principally operates in the outlook of life envisaged by the individual.

Man has, among many other things, the ratiocinating capacity, the philosophical attitude (*Jnana*), together with the

occult sense which directs him to investigate into the
phenomena that transcend the visible panorama of Nature
(*Dhyana*). He is also emotional with which sense he reacts to
God in the manner of a finite individual which feels rather
than understands the transcendent (*Bhakti*). And there are
other ways by which these reactions of soul to reality are
manifest, such as the recognition of an omnipresence in the
multitudious variety of creative activity (*Karma*). These
constitute the well-known paths of Yoga, all which converge,
in the end, as a central occupation of the consciousness
awakened to the eternal values that reign supreme in all life.

Chapter XI

THE WAY OF REASON

The Yoga of Understanding

Among the meditations that are possible, one set goes by the name of philosophical affirmations. The understanding expands itself to the dimension of a universal presence. Here, understanding is the same as meditation *(Jnana-yoga)*. To *understand* is *to be,* and *to* be is to *understand.* This does not mean the empirical intellect working through the complex of space and time, but a superior reason which overcomes these limitations, and is the presuppositon, the very background of the phenomenal intellect conditioned by space, time and causation.

Meditations Establishing the Existence of God

The limitations to which the intellect of man is subject are known by a peculiar sense in him, to designate which there is no proper word in the language. It has been often held by philosophers that the intellect is limited, that the phenomenal understanding is conditioned. But who makes this statement? How does one become aware of the limitations of one's own self? How is it possible for anyone to be aware of the logical boundaries which the intellect can reach, unless there is something which transcends the intellect, and is capable of overstepping the limitations? In deep philosophical analysis, man outgrows himself, and works through a sense which cannot be equated with the psychic operations, whether intellectual, volitional or emotional. This higher reason is the pure, illuminated understanding, to be distinguished from the ordinary understanding confined to space, time and cause. It is a presupposition which can be inferred as being there and operating, but cannot be cognised by the mental faculties. *The consciousness of finitude cannot itself be a part of the finite world.* If the consciousness of finitude were also within the finite universe, there could not be any such thing as a consciousness of finitude. *Man is aware that he is finite, and this awareness that enables him to cognise finitude is an indication of a superior element in him, which, perhaps, speaks in the language of the Infinite.*

Apart from this interesting discovery, there is also the phenomenon of change that is daily observed in the world. Everything is transitional, momentary and passing. Philosophers have never been tired of telling us that the world is a phenomenon and not the finale of things. The recognition of the fact that the world is a passing show is the act of a superior faculty, which itself cannot pass with the passing changes. Change can be seen only by a changeless something. That which changes cannot itself recognise that it changes. The contingent nature of things, or the relative character of the world, presupposes the non-contingent, or the non-conditional. This reasoning is designated as *argumentum contingentia mundi,* the argument on the basis of the contingent nature of things.

It cannot be said that the world is self-subsistent, because that which is self-sufficient and self-contained cannot aspire for transcending itself in another nature. There cannot be movement of a thing which is self-perfect. Every action, every movement, and every urge to become another thing, is to be equated with a sense of limitation felt in oneself. This urge within man, and the urge of a similar nature seen in all things, should indicate that nothing in the world is self-sufficient. Thus, the transitory nature of the world, and the restlessness characteristic of all things, should, again, be an indication of the goal of life being transcendent to things in the world, which are of the nature of an effect.

Every effect has a cause, and the nature of the effect is to move towards the cause. That the world is an effect is demonstrated by its daily movements, the very fact of the evolution of the universe. There cannot be evolution of anything, unless it is transitory and is characterised by a tendency to move to something which is beyond itself. That is why, again, it is held that the cause of the world cannot be within the world. The world is of the nature of a momentary effect; therefore the cause should be transcendent to it, which means to say that it should be outside the world,—outside, not in the sense of a spatial separation from the world, but a logical precedence. God should be logically prior to the world which is the effect. When God is said to be transcendent and beyond the world, it does not mean that God is sitting above in the skies. God's creatorship is a logical presupposition, and not a spatial transcendence, or a location in some distant atmosphere.

There is also a feeling in everyone and everything to gather more and more of status to oneself. The status in which one finds oneself is always found to be insufficient. Everything grows, and everything has a tendency to grow, to increase, and to expand. Man asks for more and more of everything, and never gets satisfied with whatever is supplied to him. This asking for a 'more' should end in a culmination, which, too, indicates that this culmination should exist. There cannot be aspiration for a thing which is nowhere. If human aspirations have a meaning, what they suggest should also have a meaning. If we feel that our aspirations actually exist and that they are not merely apparitions, then that which they seek should be there as a reality, because thought cannot operate in non-existence.

The perfection that one sees in the world, the method with which Nature works, and the precision which one can see in the operation of all things, is regarded as the teleological argument for the existence of God. The exactness, the minutiae, and the perfection with which anything in Nature works is incomparable. The beautiful arrangement of the parts into the wholeness of Nature cannot be explained unless there is something which brings about this arrangement. The parts cannot be connected together into the pattern of a whole, without a permeating presence bringing together all the parts into their completeness. One part cannot associate itself with another, because the one is different from the other. There cannot be any such thing as association of one thing with another thing in this world, there cannot be a coordination of one individual with another individual, if some element does not operate as a cementing link between things. One finds that everywhere such an association is recognisable,—in human beings, in animals, in plants, and even in inanimate structures. Everything tends towards everything else. This is what one observes everywhere. In the astronomical universe, there is the law of gravitation; in the social world, there is the law of organisation; in the mental world, there is the sanity of coherence in thought which hinges into a living whole the variety in mental functions. The principle of affection or love that one psychologically demonstrates in one's life is again an indication of the impossibility to exist without mutual relationship. How can there be relationship of anything unless there is a presupposition of that which transcends the distinctions obtaining between the parts or the individualities? This universal power of cohesion is termed God. The very existence of the universe in the way it works should be adequate demonstration of God's glory.

The fact that one is aware that someone or something is in front of oneself, proves that God exists; because the awareness of the presence of an object by a subject is made possible by the functioning of a principle which operates beyond the limitations of the subject and the object.

The Ontological Argument and Its Presuppositions

There is a poignant question which many have raised as to the way in which philosophy can contemplate God. God has been defined as Existence, and He cannot be conceived in any other manner, because to attribute to God any other characteristic would be to transfer the transitory qualities of the world to Eternity. No one can clearly say what God is. To define Him would be to limit Him to the visible nature of the world. To say anything would be to define, and to define would be to limit. Every definition is a limitation of the object defined. It segregates the characteristics of a particular object from those which do not belong to it. But there are no qualities which do not belong to God. Everything is in Him, and He is the repository or the supreme abundance of anything that can be thought of in the mind. Definition fails here, because definition limits, and God is limitless. Thus, the ontological position of God's being becomes the supreme object of meditation by consciousness, which also has an ontological status.

The idea of God in man is a mystery. It cannot be explained how this idea arises, because human nature is limited to every kind of finitude. There is nothing that does not limit man. He is hemmed in physically, psychologically, socially, and politically, and is spatio-temporally conditioned. Under these circumstances, it is unthinkable that the idea of a transcendent being should occur to him. A totally brainwashed individual cannot go outside the limits of the prescribed conditions. But there is something struggling within man even in the midst of these handicaps, which asserts relentlessly the presence of something beyond him, and which cannot be equated with anything that is seen, or heard, or even thought normally. Though the presence cannot be defined, cannot be characterised in any specified way, there is some weird haunting which keeps everyone perpetually seeking through every desire, aspiration, Or activity. Man tends to a larger and larger expansion of the area of his being through his vocations, through his thoughts, feelings and efforts, of every kind. There is only one thing that we seem to be endeavouring to achieve in life; viz., to expand the area of our existence. Dictators work hard, totalitarian governments try to impose themselves on other individuals subject to them. There is a desire to dominate over everything, a psychological fever which cannot brook any limitation imposed upon it by the existence of other finites external to it.

The idea of God is the idea of perfection, the idea of limitlessness, the idea of the infinite, the idea of the immortal, and the eternal. These ideas cannot arise under the conditions of space, time and causal limitations, the world of births and deaths. It has to be inferred by a severe logic that man does not entirely belong to the phenomenal world. He is a citizen of two realms, perhaps, partly belonging to this world, and partly to another realm which is different in order. He is not involved in phenomena wholly. Hence phenomena do not satisfy him. Else, he would have been contented with the things of the world. But nothing satisfies him. Contentment is unknown to man. No one who was wholly contented was born into this world. Man departs with a discontent. Discontentment would be unimaginable if he were to be wholly involved in the world of Nature. The asking for the unlimited, which is the main impulse in everyone, this great asking or seeking, has to arise from a source and centre which cannot belong to this world.

This novel idea has become the subject of a variety of discussions in philosophical circles. The consequences following from this idea have managed to elude the grasp of commonsense. Such an idea as this cannot be an object of sense. It does not arise by the operations of the senses in respect of the world. We do not see things and then begin to entertain this idea, because there is nothing in the world which can evoke such an idea in the mind. Nothing seen can be regarded as a source of this idea. The idea should be *a priori*, as they call it; i.e., it must be inherent in man. The things of the world cannot contribute anything to the generation of this thought in the human mind. As this idea is associated with All-Being, the Being which comprehends all things, its affirmation becomes a conscious acceptance of the totality of existence. In scriptures like the *Yoga-Vsishtha*, a type of meditation of this kind is called *Brahm-Bhavana*, which is the assertion of absoluteness free from all relative associations.

Brahman is the Absolute, and *one cannot meditate on Brahman, because it is inclusive of even the meditator himself.* Man cannot meditate on God because God includes the human location. Thus, to endeavour to meditate on the omnipresence of God would be a simultaneous attempt to abolish one's own individual existence. *When God is, man ceases to be.* This is a subtle result that would insinuate itself into the effort at meditation on the supremacy of All-Being. God, thus, ceases to be an object of individual contemplation. God is the *Supreme Subject* which contemplates Itself as the All. One, generally, regards oneself as the subject, and what is contemplated upon as the object. But in the case of God, conceived in the true sense of the term, the meditating consciousness affiliates itself with the object in such an intimate manner that in this inward association of the meditator with the object of meditation it would appear that the object itself is in a state of meditation. In a heightened form of meditation in this way, the meditating spirit enters into the body of the object with such force that it dissolves itself in the object, as rivers melt down in the ocean. In a sense, it may be said that no one is meditating on God, because that someone is a part of God's all-comprehensive Being. Then, who would do the meditation? When one goes deep into this investigative spirit, it would be realised that it is *a meditation with which God is bathing Himself.* It is God becoming conscious of Himself, or the universe getting illumined into its own self-conscious attitude. One cannot distinguish between the universe and God in the ultimate sense. The distinction has arisen on account of our maintaining an individuality of our own as physical bodies, social units, psychological egos, etc.

The *Yoga-Vasishtha* tells us that the highest form of meditation is an inward affirmation of the cosmic presence of *Brahman.* This is what is known as *Brahma-Abhyasa.* The form which the mind takes in this meditation is known as *Brahmakara-Vritti,* the psychosis which assumes the form of the cosmic substance. An ordinary psychological operation is called *Vishayakara-Vritti*, or the object-oriented psyche. In *Brahmakara-Vritti* the object outside becomes a part of the Cosmic Subject. Here, the mind assumes the largest possible status of itself. Its dimension reaches the utmost logical limits. The mind cannot exist without an object before it. The existence of the mind is the existence of the object. In fact, *the mind is only a name that is given to consciousness contemplating something outside itself.* When consciousness is aware of an object, it is called mind. The mind cannot be there if the object is not there. What happens to the mind in meditation? It gets withdrawn into consciousness. The *Vishayakara-Vritti*, or the objectified consciousness, becomes universalised consciousness, which is *Brahmakara-Vritti.* Then it no more exists as a mental function. There is no operation of any kind, because all operations are forms of externalised awareness. It is consciousness assuming a cosmic form and affirming its status as such when *Brahman* becomes its content. Since, here, consciousness has no object outside it, there is no perceptional or epistemological activity. *Consciousness is aware of itself, and in being aware of itself, it is aware of all things; and to be aware of all things is to be aware of itself (Tat-tvam-asi)*

In this comprehensive attitude of consciousness, it becomes the very principle of intelligence pervading the whole universe. This supreme principle operating everywhere is what is designated as the *Virat-Purusha*, or the *Universal Person*. In the *Bhagavadgita*, there is a description of the *Virat*, when it is told that Lord Krishna assumed the cosmic form. This is the form which consciousness takes when it permeates and enters into every fibre of creation. The universe does not any more exist as a conglomeration of particulars or as objects of sense. It stands transfigured as a whole in the totality of cosmic subjectivity. This Total Subject envisaging the Total Object is known as *Ishvara*-consciousness, or God-Awareness, the original creative performance of the

Almighty. One has to humbly try to induce into oneself this awareness in deep meditation. Meditation is our graduated participation in the consciousness of this enveloping fullness. It is achieved by degrees. The divine consciousness manifests itself in stages in the evolutionary processes of the universe. Even the little individual mind here, as a person, is a degree of that very consciousness. But here, in the case of man, it has descended to so low a state that it has identified itself with the physical form and is unable to feel its presence in other forms. The all-pervading consciousness has come down to the physical forms and has become individual bodies and objects. The lowest descent has taken such a morbid shape that it cannot recognise its kinship with the rest of the world. It has got tied up to the four walls of this tiny body and it cannot visualise itself in other such bodies. But, though it cannot consciously feel its presence in others, yet, subconsciously, or unconsciously, it is pulled towards other things, for it is, after all, present there at the invisible depths and centres of things. Consciousness cannot be destroyed, it is immortal and undividedly present. *The unconscious pull exerted by, its own presence in other things is the reason behind attractions, affections, loves and spirits of organisation in creation, from the lowest form of the gyration of the atoms, to the galaxies that spin through endless space.*

These are some of the ways of philosophical meditation and rational enquiry. There are other types of meditation still, from which all a few have been selected here as specimens of the attainments of reason, where all the faculties get gathered up into a single insight capable of an unparalleled togetherness of perception.

Stages of Knowledge

It is said in the *Yoga-Vasishtha* that in the earliest stage of knowledge, there is an inward inclination for search after truth. The stage of mind where this eagerness to search itself is not there cannot be regarded as one of any understanding. It is not believed that animals and plants have an inclination in the direction of a quest for truth. Self-consciousness, as it is available in the human level, is not supposed to be manifest in the lower kingdoms, the animal, the plant and the mineral. It is only at the human stage that discrimination is supposed to dawn, because self-consciousness is at the same time a capacity to discriminate and distinguish between what is proper and what is improper, and what is real and what is unreal. But it does not mean that every human being is in search of truth. When one speaks of a human being the reference is to the species. The anthropological study of mankind will reveal that it is not true that everyone belonging to the human species is in a uniform state of awareness. While all can be regarded as men, some are, in fact, animal-men. They think like animals, though they have two legs and they belong to the human species. The animal-man is perhaps the state of the *homo sapiens* risen immediately above the animal level with traces of the animal still left, and at that stage man thinks like the beast with an intensity of selfishness gone to the extreme, with a desire to grab and destroy and consume and with no consideration for others absolutely. This is the lowest state in which man can be evaluated. But there are superior individuals who have risen above the animal level, yet are intensely selfish nevertheless, who may be good to anyone only if the other is good to them, but bad if the other is bad to them. They are men of the 'tit-for-tat' attitude, and, here, again, the turbidity of the mind persists. But man has to rise to the still higher level where he metes out only good to the other and cognises not the bad element. *The good man is one who does good always, under every condition, and is not conditionally good. Beyond the good man is the saintly man, and still above, the Godman,* whatever be our description of such a state of illumination.

It is only in the later stages of evolution that the spirit of search rises and fructifies in experience, firstly as a wish to be good. This is regarded as the first stage in knowledge. When man is not satisfied with the things of the world, when he begins to feel that there is something missing here, and that there ought to be a state of living superior to the earthly forms of life, and is eager to know what is behind this world, then he is in the first stage of knowledge *(Subhechha)*.

When the enquiring spirit dawns, one does not merely rest with this spirit, he tries to work for its manifestation in practical life. One would run about here and there and try to find out how he can materialise this longing and make it a part of his living routine. Man, then, becomes a philosopher. A philosopher is in the second stage of knowledge *(Vicharana)*. He employs his reasoning capacity and works through his logical acumen, trying to make sense out of this inward spirit of search for truth, and he utilises his whole life in study and analysis of the nature of things.

In the third stage, man becomes a truly spiritual seeker. He does not remain a professor of philosophy or an academic seeker in the metaphysical sense, but a seeker in the practical field. He begins to practise knowledge and does not remain merely in a state of searching for it. The mind is gradually thinned out of all its jarring elements and it recognises no value in life except a unitive insight into truth. Practice is the motto of the seeker. He *does* things, and is not content to *imagine* them. This is the third stage of knowledge where one starts actually doing things, because he has already risen above the state of conceptualisation, rational study and philosophising. The mind is thinned out of desires for the external *(Tanumanasi)*.

The fourth stage of knowledge is supposed to be that state when there are flashes of the divine light appearing before the meditative consciousness like streaks of lightning *(Sattvapatti)*. It is not a continued vision, but a passing state of exaltation. A flash does not continue for a long time. It manifests itself suddenly for a second and then vanishes as an intense beam of light. This is the fourth state of consciousness, regarded as the first stage of realisation.

The fourth stage of knowledge mentioned is considered to be the initial indication of God coming. The earlier three are only stages of search and practice. The fourth is the first encounter with the supermundane. The condition of this first stage of realisation or the fourth stage of knowledge is designated as the condition of the *Brahmavit,* or knower of reality, where one begins to see, actually, what is there, rather than merely think intellectually or imagine in the mind.

Then the fifth stage is described as a higher realm still, where on account of the immense joy one experiences beyond description, one is automatically detached from all objective contacts of sense *(Asamsakti).* One does not 'practise' renunciation here. One is spontaneously relieved of all longings in the same way as when one wakes up from dream there is no longing for the wealth of the dream world. There are no more realities outside, even as the objects of dream are no more realities to one who is awake.

In the sixth stage, the seeking soul becomes a Godman, a veritable divinity moving on earth, where the world is no more before him but the blaze of the all-enveloping creative spirit spread out in its splendour and glory. He sees the substance of the world and not merely the form and the name. He beholds the forms but as constituting a single interconnected whole. The veil of Space and time is lifted. The conditioning factors, earlier known as space, time and cause, and the internal empirical relationships, get transcended. One enters into the heart of all things, the selfhood of every being. Light commingles with light. As a candle flame may join a candle flame, the self gets attuned to the Universal Self. Here it is not a beholding through the senses or even a thinking by the mind, but *being, as such.* The materiality of the world vanishes *(Padarthabhavana).* The world then shines as a radiance and as delight. Earlier it was iron, now it is gold. The world does not really vanish, but it has become now a different thing. It has no form, it is a mass of brilliance. The objectness of the objects has gone; the externality of things is no more; space and time do not exist; one does not 'see' things, for one has 'become' things. And, still, there is a higher communion.

The seventh stage is not a stage of beholding anything at all. There is no beholder any more. The seer is not dissociated from the seen. There is nothing to act as a bar or a distinguishing line between the subject and the object. The universe no more stands there as an object of experience, it is the Subject of All-Experience. Here, the Universal Spirit is what it is; none is there to know it, or experience it. It is experience pure, it is experience itself, not an experience 'of' something. Nothing can be said about it, for there is none to say anything. This is the final attainment (*Turiya*).

The seventh stage is also called, sometimes, 'liberation while living' (*Jivanmukti*). The body may be there, but it is no more a body for the knower. What a liberated soul feels, no one else can understand. There is no standard by which one can judge that person. The state is beyond imagination. What happens to the soul in liberation, one has no means to measure or convey. The Goal of life is reached.

Chapter XII

THE SYSTEM OF YOGA

Patanjali's Prescriptions for Meditation in Life

Meditations which are more occult in nature consist mainly in the exercise of the will, charged with a determined understanding. This system, too, has a philosophical basis, though it takes an intensely practical turn when the exercise commences. This type of meditation is psychic in the beginning though spiritual in the end; a process by which one places oneself in a closer affinity with the objects of the world. By continued habituation to the subsisting relationship between oneself and the things of the world one gets into their substance and, in a sense, embraces the very roots of objectivity. The meditational techniques prescribed in the *Yoga Sutras* of *Patanjali* border upon a cosmic association of oneself with objects, stage by stage, commencing with particular things chosen for the purpose of meditation, and gradually expanding the area of action into other objects, culminating in the concentration of consciousness on that great reservoir of all things, the universe of elements and forces.

The object of meditation is generally regarded by novitiates as some isolated, individual, localised unit with no connection with other units, or other locations. That it is mostly taken to be so has been observed often in our earlier studies. This is the normal way of human appreciation. The segmentation of object is caused by a notion in the mind, according to which the object is a point of definition, by which act of characterisation, definitions which apply to other objects do not apply to this particular concerned object. The mind associates name and form with objects. It cannot think, conceive, or visualise an object as it is in itself. The objects, when they are presented to human perception and cognition, are already conditioned by these associations, viz., *name* and *form.*

There is a form given to the object of concentration. The form is a peculiar nexus of composition which distinguishes it from other forms. In fact, the *differentia* which isolates from other objects the particular point of concentration is the complex of formation,—*Rupa,* the network of definition. But the mistake lies in the position that the form itself is taken to be the object. The metaphysical essence of the object is identified with the phenomenal form with which it is invested, and this identification is made worse by another imagination that it exists in its own status and bears no relation with others.

It was observed that the universe is an organism and not a society of isolated fragments. As it does not constitute an assemblage of differentiated parts but stands unified within itself, the empirical notion of the object cannot bear the test of deeper investigation. There is a basic error in the very act of sensory perception. The inward organic relationship which obtains between things at their back does not become the object of perception. What is cognised is only the form. It is difficult to explain the intricate involvements which contribute to the very subsistence of this name-form complex of the object. The form of the object is a temporary abstraction from a larger possibility of which also it is capable, but of which it is divested due to the particular intentions and abilities of the observing principle, observer, the percipient, or, rather, the desires of the individual. There are researches which have concluded that the constitution of a particular object does not merely depend on the nature of the relationship to a percipient, but it also depends much on its own individual appetitions. The status which an object occupies, the form which it assumes and even the relationship it bears to others, are all determined by the basic affirmative force which maintains its given complex-form. The object is just this much, viz., the name-form nexus. One has to stretch the imagination somewhat to understand what all this means.

The secret of this way of interpreting the structure of objects is in the foundations of the *Samkhya* system of analysis, which, with some modifications, is now being propounded in the fields of present-day science. The pioneers in modern physics have come to the conclusion that the object so-called is not an *existent* something, but an *abstraction,*—and the meaning of this word has to be clear to us. An abstraction is a philosophical concept by which what is intended is the segregation of a specific group of characters from the infinite possibilities of the universe by shutting out all such possibilities for the sake of a tentative convenience or a necessity arising out of a type of affirmation of individuality, which is what is called the 'object'. While there is an infinitude of resources at the background, there is a vast sea of potentials, one does not wish to present oneself as a sea, but would like to be projected as a percentage of the possibilities of this vastness, and become, for all practical purposes, one among the many and not the only one that is at the source. The analogy of the waves in the ocean is well known, but it does not explain the matter fully, because every wave is like every other wave in its essence. Though the size, the force, or the shape of a wave may differ from those of other waves, the quintessential base of one wave is the same as that of other waves. But, here, in the case of the objects that are being contemplated in this fashion, the case is different. One object is not like another object. There is an essential difference in the very structure of the objects, which arises on account of the difference in the nature of the self-affirmation, the central force, or the nucleus of the individuality, which is in every object, and which isolates itself, and has to isolate itself, from other such centres of affirmation, for its most surprising non-altruistic satisfaction.

One ego differs from another ego in the intensity of its assertion and also in the form of its assertion. An object is a centre of egoism, and this egoism, again, must be understood in its philosophical connotation, rather than in the social form which is generally associated with it. The ego as the subject of philosophical analysis is not the pride that is normally thought to be its feature. It is not the arrogance of social authority. The ego is an urge to maintain oneself as distinct from others. In the Yoga texts the term used is *Asmita,* the sense of 'I am'-ness. This affirmation of the 'I am', or the 'me', is the basis of one being different from another.

In the act of meditation, what is attempted is to break this barrier of the object by removing its affirmative demarcation characterising it as a form, or object, and entering into the essential presupposition of the very affirmation causing the presentation of objectness. Thus, in an act of single concentration, the meditative consciousness probes into the root of the object and thereby also comprehends the essence of every other object in the world.

In the system of *Patanjali,* there is a type of concentration that he prescribes among many others, viz., the breaking of the knot of objectivity by means of separating the essence of the object from the form which it has assumed and also the name which designates it, or defines it. *Nama, Rupa* and *Tattva,* name, form and reality are the temporal and metempirical phases of everything in creation.

Name: The Designation of the Object

Every object is defined by certain characterisations. The definitions form the name of the object. The name is a verbal or conceptual symbol of the features which constitute the object. In the Indian tradition, the naming of a person is regarded as an important ritual in the career of life. Any and every name cannot be given to a person. The name of the person indicates the character of that person, the pattern of the individuality of that person, and it almost describes the person. The description of the behaviour of the individuality of the object is the name of that object. The name or the description has become a necessity in the case of the object because of the form that it has assumed either in relation to the percipient or on account of the special affirmative character of its own basic root, the ego.

The preliminary stage of meditation is a contemplation on the object associated with name and form,—the designation, the description or the characterisation of the object, even if it be a conceptual object, plus the idea of its form. It will be found that a thing is invariably associated with an idea about it proceeding from the subject of cognition, and a description of it by which it is separated from other objects. An inward characterisation of the object isolates the particular object from other objects. This is what is called the naming of the object. And there is at the same time a concept of the object which is a more subtle and deeper isolation of the very existence of the object from the existence of other objects. Even if the whole universe is to be regarded as a total object of meditation, it will be conditioned by these invariable concomitants of cognition. Nothing can be imagined without being described in some such way. The name that is associated with the universe is, however, a purely psychological convenience and not necessarily a proper picturing of its nature. No word need be uttered in language in respect of an object, and yet it gets characterised in the minds of observers. This is the strange predicament in which one gets involved in the very act of perception of anything, from which extrication is hardly achieved.

The focussing of the attention of consciousness on the chosen object, whether it is an isolated thing or the whole universe, associating it with *name* and *form*, is an invariable step in meditation. This is regarded as the first step, though it is hard enough for a novitiate even to conceive it.

What does concentration do? The thing-in-itself, the object as it is, is attempted to be separated from the complexities in which it is involved, the *form* and the *name*. There is no necessity to go into the more philosophical meaning of all these issues. Simple examples may be taken to make the matter a little clear. Truly, no one has a name. One is *Rama,* another is *Krishna;* one is *Jack* and another is *John.* But these are only conventions and not realities in themselves. The particular name by which an individual is defined is not actually necessary for the existence of that individual. One can live even without that name. If a man were to live alone somewhere, the name would have no meaning for him. Nobody is going to call him, and it is not necessary that he should look upon himself or think of himself as a particular name. The name of an individual loses significance when there is no need to establish a social relationship with others. The need for social contact may be regarded as one of the reasons behind the naming of things. In fact, man stands alone in the world and, therefore, he can stand without a name. Imagine yourself as seated in an isolated place, with no one to see you and with no one to contact; what is there in your name then? And also, when you were born into this world, you did not bring with you any name. You have no name in actuality. It should, then, be easy to give up thinking in terms of names.

Thus, one should achieve a state of matter-of-fact understanding as far as the name is concerned. Even as man need not have a name, anything in the world also need have no name. Things can be without name, though a necessity is felt for naming them in order to recognise them, describe them and associate them with other such objects, and distinguishing them. But, as such, there is not always such an emergency to describe things and associate them or differentiate them.

This satisfaction would be to take one step as an advance in the way of meditation on the chosen ideal. Objects must be dissociated from their names and looked upon as they would be without characterisation by name. Do not call the tree as a tree. Decondition your mind by entering into the concept of the form of the tree without bringing in the name, or the word, 'tree'. We are so much familiar with names, and so much engrossed in their reality that we would not find this an easy affair. We cannot think of a tree without imagining that it is a tree, verbally also. It requires a little bit of the power of the will backed up with a sustained understanding, the understanding that there is no need to name an object. Objects have really no name. This is a clear understanding, and there should be no difficulty about it. If the understanding is stable, the will would take care of itself.

The concentration on an object, a tree, or any such thing, should be a mutual contact of the *pure subject* with the *pure objectivity* of that on which one concentrates. As the object need not have a name, we, too, human beings, have no name. It is not a Mr. So-and-so concentrating on something called by such-and-such a name. The first step in this meditation is to dissociate oneself from one's own name and also the object from its appended name. This initial step would be a difficult thing, since no one can normally dissociate oneself from one's name and station. It is known that when we are fast asleep, we would not wake up if we are called by another person's name. Even in sleep the name manages to become an organic part of one's individuality. Such is one's attachment to name. If *Rama* is sleeping, he must be called as *Rama* only. If you call him *Gopal,* he would not awake. Even in sleep the person is *Rama,* the name. Look at the force of attachment! We are bundles of such entanglements, and *Yoga* is all detachment. We cannot believe ourselves to be anything other than what the name indicates.

Form: The Nexus of Objective Centralisation

But this is not enough, says *Patanjali,* the master of *Yoga.* Though the dissociation of the object from its name and the dissociation of one's own self from one's own name is essential and is difficult enough, there is something more difficult ahead, viz., the dissociation of the object from its form. The form is not the essence of the object, just as the body is not man's soul. When we see ourselves, we look upon this body that is six feet in height. This physical frame is not our essentiality. Likewise, the form is not the essence of the object. The second step is more difficult than the earlier one. While the de-naming of a thing is hard indeed, the de-forming of it is still more difficult, because everyone lives in a world of forms. We see nothing but forms in the world. How could one go above the normal?

Here, one can be a little philosophical, again. As there is an interrelatedness of everything with everything else in this organic structure of the universe, it would be futile to imagine that any object has an independent form of its own. This is a more mature way in which one can convince oneself that objects have no form of their own. Hence, they cannot also have a name. When there is no form, how can there be a name? Profounder studies would convince us that the universe is made in such a way that everything is related to everything else, internally. Thus, there cannot be an isolated form for any part of the structure. There cannot also be a name to any such abstracted part. Name and form drop out altogether. The idea of the object and the description of the object are phenomenal associations from which the essence of the object has to be freed entirely. The pure object, or the *artha,* as it is called, has to shine in its own pristine purity. The subject has to behold the object as it is in its own status, not as it appears to the complex of the perceptual faculties. Objects are involved in space, time and the relativity of things. The space-time-cause complex is what is called the form of the object. Hence the form is a metaphysical entity, and it cannot be pierced through by any phenomenal faculty of man, such as the sense-oriented mind or the logic-ridden intellect. One has to sink down into one's metaphysical root in order to be able to encounter, befriend and break through the form. The subject and the object are on a parallel level of reality at every degree of their formation, depth or constituency. *Yoga* is not for the careless and the non-vigilant.

Difficulties in the Meditational Technique

The object is a knot of individualisation in the infinite net of the universe. The knot, which is the object, has to break, because the object is nothing but a tied up force. It is a tie, a *Granthi,* as the occult *Yoga* scriptures sometimes define the object. These *granthis,* or knots, are, again of a complicated nature. The object is not merely one knot, but a heaped-up pile of several knots. The difficulty can well be imagined when one has to try to untie a heap of knots into which a rope is hardened at a point. One has to untie one, then another, and then a third one, and so on, one after another, slowly, the outermost having to be tackled first in the attempt.

In a mysterious way, adepts in *Yoga* have held that there are mainly three *Granthis,* or knots, by which a particular formation is driven into the context of what is called an object,—*Brahma-granthi, Vishnu-granthi* and *Rudra-granthi. Brahma, Vishnu* and *Siva* are supposed to be the presiding deities of these knots, by which what is intended seems to be that the creative, preservative and transforming forces are involved in the presence of any object. Every moment the object is created, every moment it is sustained, and every moment it is destroyed. This is what is meant by saying that *Brahma, Vishnu* and *Siva* are ruling the universe, which is just a flood-tide of forms.

These *Granthis* are, actually, not three different knots. Hence this knot is more difficult to handle than the ordinary rope-knots that one can see with one's eyes. One may untie the rope from its knots, because they seem to be one over the other in layers. But the processes of creation, preservation and destruction are *not heaped* one over the other. They *are involved,* one in the other. Here is all the difficulty. The one is not outside the other, nor does one follow the other in succession. It does not mean that today there is creation, tomorrow preservation, the day after, destruction. *Brahma, Vishnu* and *Siva* act simultaneously. There is a kind of mutual dependence in the acts of creation, preservation and transformation. *The objects of the world are intricate networks, asserting their centre of isolation on the one hand, and consisting of nothing more than the shape taken by pressurised points of cosmical relativity and dependence, on the other. Subjects and objects are of the visible world and also of realms which touch the infinitude of existence. The temporal and the eternal are both preset in all things. Yoga is* concerned with this dual encounter with the object of meditation.

Intense Aspiration and Tenacity in Practice Are Necessary

While it is practically impossible for the uninitiated student to visualise the whole object of meditation, it is equally difficult to engage oneself wholly, even in any occupation in life. Here is an insight into how life can be a *Yoga.* The difficulty is that one cannot concentrate on anything for a continued duration, and it matters not whether it is a limited centre or a large object. The problem is purely inward, psychological and an incapacity to attend to anything with the soul in it. Man requires change. The mind asks for variety, and to feed it with a single thing always would be a futile exercise. Let one try to contemplate any form or concept continuously for several minutes, one will find that it is not possible. At the time of this attempt for the fixing of attention, it will be found that the mind subtly contemplates other characters also. The finite has been accustomed to seek joy in finite presentations alone. Education is not always pleasant.

The effort that is necessary in this direction is rightly described as superhuman. The involvements of the human personalities are so intricate and almost beyond imagination that, ordinarily, success may not show its head even after years of practice. But persistent effort will have its own results. Says *Patanjali:* "Success is imminent in the case of those whose ardour and tenacity are supernormal; *(Tivrasamveganamasannah).* Everyone has some sort of an aspiration: 'I wish to be liberated', so does everybody feel at heart. Well, one may like to be liberated, but who bothers about a mere statement? Where is the effort for its fulfilment?

Due to the complexity of the nature of 'objectivity' in which everything is involved, including our own selves, we have to take sufficient time to tackle the situation. It may require some guidance from a competent teacher; else, who can understand all these hard things? Our minds are poor, our intelligence is turbid, our will is weak, and our flesh has its own say even though the spirit may be willing.

A great tenacity is called for in meditation. In the beginning the problems are common with any student. But they get obviated stage by stage by continued practice. The essence of Yoga is practice (Abhyasa). There is not much use in reading a lot or gathering information in an academic sense. What is required is application of will and a protracted, persistent effort with daily sessions of meditation, and by prolonging the duration of meditation as days pass. There should be a systematised intensity of practice for years, and not merely for a few months or days. While for some years one's whole life may have to be spent in this discipline, one will slowly realise that one has no other duty in this world. All our well-intentioned occupations in life are the little cries of the central longing of the soul for freedom untrammelled. The world's usual ways have to be brought together into this pivotal enterprise of the wholeness of personality for an utter liberation by a sinking of oneself in the Absolute. We may have to harmonise our other occupations with this cosmical aspiration of all life. There should be no conflict between the calls of daily life and the centrality of the world's main purpose. Man is his best teacher, finally. No external guide can help him in the end. It is he that has to tread the path, and somebody else cannot walk for him. But, one is never alone, for the world is an eternal associate, and all creation rises in joy at the prospects of participating in the blessed attainment.

The Yoga Way of Life

Yoga is the science of life. In the practice of Yoga, as it is in the process of general education, five elements are necessarily involved,—the teacher, 'the taught (student), the aim, the subject and the method. The study of Yoga being an important process in the education of the human being, these factors invariably come into play in one's attempt at its practice. In the field of this important endeavour on the part of the human being, there is often-times no success because of a lack of clarity among these essentials of study. Most persons forget these elementals of educational psychology and do not achieve anything substantial.

The most important factor in the process is the teacher, more than even the study. The nature and competency of the teacher plays the primary role in the Yoga system, and what we need today is a proper teacher of the subject. Teachers have either no interest in the students or their knowledge is inadequate and does not fit into the context of the student. One of the main characteristics of a teacher is that he has really to feel what he speaks, and live, to a large extent, what he teaches. Only then does the teaching become effective. Good teachers speak not merely by words but by their lives. Due to a disharmony between the inner and outer life of the teacher, there may come about a failure of his efforts. The second qualification of a good teacher is that he should be able to understand the student even more than the subject. He should teach what the student needs. The speaking is done to a person or persons and not to walls or to the hall. He should not say either more or less than what the student would expect in his present state of mind. Thirdly, there must be a force in the teaching, and the force has naturally to come from the teacher himself and not from his studies, or even the nature of the subject. The teacher is a living being and his presence itself has an effect of its own on the student. One is inspired more by listening than by reading. The teacher's role is indeed primary.

But, what about the student? The student does not play any less important role. Unless there is reception, the teaching will vanish into the air. Whatever has been imparted should not be conducted into the earth but absorbed into the proper medium. The competent student is one who has no other interest than the subject of study. Due to diffusion of energy on account of extraneous interests, putting one's nose in such distractions as communal or political affairs, etc., and also due to personal problems, the teaching may not be received properly. If the student is worried, vexed, etc., the teaching cannot be received. The teacher and the taught are like the right and left hand of a person, and the two form a harmonious movement in which knowledge is revealed. The student, therefore, should be competent enough to receive knowledge by freeing himself from complexities and problems and fixing his heart in the subject. With these conditions fulfilled, the aim of study becomes clear.

The aim of Yoga is not always easy to understand. Many entertain a wrong notion of it and misunderstand it. What is the purpose behind the practice of Yoga? It is accepted to be the achievement of perfection. Yoga is a process not merely of reaching the highest, but also of bringing a sense of perfection even in small things such as one's office work or profession. *Perfection is Yoga* in any field of life, or in any vocation. Yoga makes one a perfect person. But it is only a few who want perfection in anything. While many would like to fulfil their desires, perfection is something they cannot understand. The attempt to fulfil desires is the opposite of perfection. *Perfection is balance and harmony in life,* while desire is a disbalance of thought. Yoga is a system of striking a balance, firstly with persons and things outside, and later in one's own being,—in the physical, vital, psychological, intellectual and spiritual levels. The basic instruction of Patanjali in this regard is *Yama* and *Niyama.* These fundamentals are attempts to establish harmony between the society and in the layers of one's own being. If you are discordant in yourself, you cannot be at peace with yourself, much less with others. You will only create an atmosphere of unhappiness wherever you go, for, in yourself, you are unwell. The reason behind the requirement of striking a harmony in the practice of Yoga is that the world is a harmony, the universe is a harmony, God is harmony, the Absolute is harmony, and to be in tune with it in every respect would be Yoga. Nature does not fight with itself; it is man who does the fighting. When man learns to be in harmony with Nature, it is the first stage of Yoga.

Why does man fret and fume and struggle and oppose? Because he is selfish, he has a craving for satisfying his senses and he is anxious about it, while in fact, happiness is of Nature in its simplicity. Harmony is the name for happiness, and is known as *Sáttva*. Agitation is *Rajas* and absence of initiative is *Tamas*. The more you approximate yourself to a balance of forces, the more are you near to Yoga. If you are able to understand others, if you can enter into the feelings of those around you, you are going to be a socially successful person. The world, in a way, is a reflection of what you are, in the mirror of your mind. What you think about the world, the world thinks about you; what you do to the world, the world does to you. The reaction from the world is exactly what you do to it. This is a psychological secret which a student of Yoga fully understands. He does not react, but understands, with great patience. As a matter of fact, there would be no reaction from a student of Yoga, because understanding absorbs everything into itself, and so the question of reaction does not arise. If you throw a ball against a wall, it will bump back, but space will absorb it. The student of Yoga is capable of receiving all the buffets of the world, because these do not come to him as reactions in respect of him. When you change yourself within, the world will correspondingly change itself in respect of you. This is the basic, requisite understanding in Yoga. Yoga is not mere exercises, though it is also exercises; it is not a mechanical repetition of some routine but a spirit evolved into life. All this has to be learnt from a teacher, and it calls for an intimate touch between teaching and learning. The system of *Gurukulavasa,* which is the system of learning from the teacher, by living with him, was followed in ancient India. Here the *Guru* guides the student like a parent. The aim of Yoga can fructify only in such an atmosphere.

Now, we come to the subject of Yoga. What do we study in Yoga? It is not a book that we have merely to read but a subject of which the books are only embodiments. Why do you go to, and what do you want from, Yoga? Just as you go to a shop to purchase what you need, you go to Yoga because you lack something which is not available in the world. You want Yoga because you have some difficulties which the world cannot solve. You may have plenty of wealth, and a good position in society; and yet you may not be peaceful. Something seems to be wrong somewhere. Something is stinking in some corner, though outwardly it is all wonderful to see with the eyes. Though the aim of Yoga is universal, its practice is an individual affair, and not a social one, because everyone's difficulty is peculiar to oneself alone. Everyone is equally hungry, but each one requires a different type of diet. Though the longing is the same, the way of fulfilment varies. So, the teaching differs in detail and in emphasis. Question yourself: 'What is wrong with me?'. Those who do not understand what is wanting in them may approach and ask of their superiors. Though the reason for one's deficiency may be at variance with that of another, one thing seems to be in common,—there is no true and lasting happiness in life. No one can always be happy. But, why? Yoga may be said to be the quest for permanent happiness. There is no peace, and we want peace. How does Yoga bring happiness and peace?

The aim of Yoga is the setting up of a balance or harmony and not judging another from one's own standpoint. Art brings joy, because it is beautiful, and it is beautiful because it is balance, rhythm, system, arrangement and because it gives us a proportion which our soul receives with a kinship of feeling. The soul is balance, and it feels happy in meeting balance from outside, like a friend meeting a friend. This is also why sensory satisfaction brings a temporary happiness, and why, though it is condemned by the wise, people run after it. When the senses come in contact with objects, they bring a sort of satisfaction caused by this harmony risen on account of a cessation of mental distraction in the form of desire. The harmony of feeling is the kinship represented to the soul within, and it is overjoyed. Also there is a correspondence of structure between a sense and its object. This correspondence, again, is harmony. The sense-satisfaction is not permanent, because (i) you cannot have the object always,—either it goes away or you yourself pass away; and (ii) the object has not really brought the harmony,—the harmony was due to absence of desire, the balance being brought about within by the contact which acted only as a medium. Yoga teaches us how to attain eternal happiness by setting up a balance in us permanently, while the external object gives only a temporary delight. Yoga is an independent effort unconnected with transient objects. Yoga brings happiness even without persons or things around you, even when you are alone. The Yogin wants nothing because his happiness depends not on anything outside. A proper psychological adjustment of oneself with Reality is the great end of Yoga, and when this is achieved, a conscious happiness, identical with all existence, manifests itself. Perfect happiness is a perfect state of consciousness, and the subject of Yoga consists of all those concessions and adjustments, inclusions and exclusions, externally as well as internally, which are necessary to build up that mysterious and yet unavoidable wholeness in life,—*universal harmony*.

The method is the actual process of practice, as explained herein. It is really high time now to act with wisdom and caution and do something positive rather than pursue the old habit of seeing just defect only in others. There uare many causes of today's unhappy situation in the world,—of anxiety, partisanism, exploitation and violence of various kinds. An effort towards the moral and cultural regeneration of those who cannot even think rightly, and whose intellectual Judgments and value-assessments are founded on the whims of emotions and the passions of the senses, is difficult of achievement without remedying the root of the illness. More than the lack of morals, etiquette and culture, which is in the form of an effect, there is the malady of wrong understanding and false judgment, which is the cause. The selfish individual is unconsciously working not only against others but more so against his own self under the clouded notion that it brings good. A standard of reference, which is cosmically applicable, has to act as the norm and the principle of a properly guided life.

On the basis of this impartial principle, all have to work in the different walks of life, without the untrue distinction of the superior and the inferior, in the mutually adjusted and adapted living machinery of human society. Language creed, cult, colour, power-politics and bigoted ideology should not come in the way of the implementation and realisation of this sublime aim of life in general. We have to gird up our loins and work hard for this goal, which is at once personal, social, national, international and universal.

effort towards the moral and cultural regeneration of those who cannot even think rightly, and whose intellectual judgments and value-assessments are founded on the whims of emotions and the passions of the senses, is difficult of achievement without remedying the the root of the illness. More than the lack of morals, etiquette and culture, which is in the form of an effect, there is the malady of wrong understanding and false judgment which is the cause. The selfish individual is unconsciously working not only against others but more so against his own self under the clouded notion that it brings good. A standard of reference which is cosmically applicable, has to act as the norm and the principle of a properly guided life.

On the basis of this impartial principle, all have to work in the different walks of life, without the undue distinction of the superior and the inferior, in the gradually adjusted and adapted living machinery of human society. Language, creed, cult, colour, power-politics and biased ideology, should not come in the way of the implementation and realisation of this sublime aim of life in general. We have to gird up our loins and work hard for this goal, which is at once personal, social, national, international and universal.

APPENDIX

PRACTICAL HINTS ON SPIRITUAL LIVING

1. First of all, there should be a clear conception of the Aim of one's life.

2. The Aim should be such that it should not be subject to subsequent change of opinion or transcendence by some other thought, feeling or experience. It means, the Aim should be ultimate, and there should be nothing beyond that.

3. It will be clear that, since the ultimate Aim is single, and set clearly before one's mind, everything else in the world becomes merely an instrument, an auxiliary or an accessory to the fulfilment of this Aim.

4. It is possible to make the mistake that only certain things in the world are aids in the realisation of one's Aim of life, and that others are obstacles. But this is not true; because everything in the world is interconnected and it is not possible to divide the necessary from the unnecessary, the good from the bad, etc., except in a purely relative sense. The so-called unnecessary items or the useless ones are those whose subtle connection with our central purpose in life is not clear to our minds. This happens when our minds are carried away by sudden emotions or spurts of enthusiasm.

5. All this would mean that it is not advisable or practicable to ignore any aspect of life totally, as if it is completely irrelevant to the purpose of one's life. But here begins the difficulty in the practice of Sadhana, because it is not humanly possible to consider every aspect of a situation when one tries to understand it.

6. There are economic and material needs as well as vital longings of the human nature which have to be paid their

due, at the proper time and in the proper proportion, not with the intention of acquiring comfort and satisfaction to one's self, but with a view to the sublimation of all personal desires or urges, whether physical, vital or psychological. An utter ignorance of this fact may prove to be a sort of hindrance in one's further practice on the path of Sadhana.

7. It is, of course, necessary that one should live a life of reasonable seclusion under the guidance of a master until such time when one can stand on one's own legs and think independently without any aid from anyone.

8. But, one should, now and then, test one's ability to counteract one's reactions to the atmosphere even when one is in the midst of intractable and irreconcilable surroundings. Seclusion should not mean a kind of self-hypnotism or hibernation and an incapacity to face the atmosphere around.

9. Svadhyaya does not mean study of any book that one may find anywhere at any time. It means a continued and regular study, daily, of selected holy texts, or even a single text, from among those that have been suggested above. A study in this manner, done at a fixed time, every day, for a fixed duration, will bring the expected result.

10. The Japa of the Mantra should, in the beginning, be done with a little sound in the mouth so that the mind may not go here and there towards different things. The loud chant of the Mantra will bring the mind back to the point of concentration. Later on, the Japa can be only with movement of lips, but without making any sound. In the end, the Japa can be only mental, provided that the mind does not wander during the mental Japa.

11. A convenient duration, say, half an hour, or one hour, should be set up at different times, so that the daily Sadhana should be at least for three hours a day, and not less. It can be increased according to one's capacity, as days pass.

12. During Japa, the mind should think of the meaning of the Mantra, the surrender of oneself to the Deity of the

Mantra, and finally, the communion of oneself with that Great Deity. Effort should be put forth to entertain this deep feeling during Japa, every day.

13. Meditation can be either combined with Japa, or it can be independent of Japa. Meditation with Japa means the mental repetition of the Mantra and, also, at the same time, meditation deeply on the meaning of the Mantra, as mentioned above.

14. Meditation without Japa is a higher stage where the mind gets so much absorbed in the thought of God, surrender to God and union with God, that in this meditation Japa automatically stops. This is the highest of Meditation.

15. Throughout one's Sadhana, it is necessary to feel the oneness of oneself and the universe with God.